Let's Go Fishin'

Let's Go Fishin'

It's a Beautiful Day

Donna Blair Patterson

RESOURCE *Publications* · Eugene, Oregon

LET'S GO FISHIN'
It's a Beautiful Day

Resource Publications
An Imprint of Wipf and Stock Publishers
199 W. 8th Ave., Suite 3
Eugene, OR 97401

www.wipfandstock.com

PAPERBACK ISBN: 979-8-3852-3933-7
HARDCOVER ISBN: 979-8-3852-3934-4
EBOOK ISBN: 979-8-3852-3935-1
VERSION NUMBER 01/21/25

This book is dedicated to my son who is so much like his grandfather, but he never got to meet him. Now, through this book, he will know him well.

Contents

Chapter 1: The River Calls | 1

Chapter 2: Thanks to the Oil Boom | 4

Chapter 3: And Then There Was Love | 6

Chapter 4: A New Home | 8

Chapter 5: And Then Came TV | 10

Chapter 6: You Can Write That Up | 12

Chapter 7: Big Sandy Creek | 13

Chapter 8: Notes on Pond and Fish | 16

Chapter 9: The Little Frogs | 23

Chapter 10: Bait Casting | 29

Chapter 11: The Magic Spoon | 36

Chapter 12: Synthetic Dragon | 43

Chapter 13: Fly Fishing | 50

Chapter 14: Susquehanna "Salmon" | 60

Chapter 15: Spring Fever | 64

Chapter 16: Queen of the Water | 68

Chapter 17: Wrong Way Plugging | 73

Chapter 18: Pennsylvania Muskellunge | 77

Chapter 19: Crawdads | 81

Chapter 20: Carp—Our Problem Child | 85

Chapter 21: Fly Rod Frequency | 89

Chapter 22: Curiosity | 92

Chapter 23: Pat and Mike and the Rainbow Trout | 99

CONTENTS

Chapter 24: Weedless Bass Bug | 102

Chapter 25: Weeds or Fish | 105

Chapter 26: MUD! | 108

Chapter 27: A Drop of Water | 112

Chapter 28: Our Northern Pike | 116

Chapter 29: The Last Day | 120

Chapter 30: It Happened This Way | 127

CHAPTER 1

The River Calls

"Hey Sis, let's go fishin."

"OK, Dad."

So, we grabbed our gear, climbed into the old Chevy station wagon, and headed down the road to a nearby trout stream. That was a regular part of many summer days when I was a kid.

I was the younger of two kids in our house. My sister was Judith (Judy) Ann. She was almost ten years older than me, which is why I was never expected. Everyone just called me, Sis, instead of my name, Donna. However, I was named after my dad, Donald Burnett Blair.

The story goes that Dr. Butters, who delivered me, told my mom, Helen, to name me after Dad because I would be the last baby she ever had. Seems that, when I came along, Mom thought she was "going through the change" because she was thirty-nine years old then. Family members called me an "oops" or an "aw shit", but Mom always said I was just a wonderful surprise. But enough about me.

My dad, Don Blair, was born in 1905 in a house near the Allegheny River in the small town of Franklin, Pennsylvania. His mother was Eleanora (Nora) Nelson Blair, a petite, smart, and industrious woman who went on to accomplish some great things in her own right. His father was Homer Reuben Blair, an attorney who specialized in corporate law. He traveled often by train to the big city of Pittsburgh, Pennsylvania, sixty miles south, where he worked with some of the larger steel mills at the time.

Don was an only child. His younger brother died shortly after birth when Don was two years old. The problem was not known back then, but now we refer to it as the Rh factor. Today it is identified and handled so that babies survive. Unfortunately, back in 1907, the baby died.

Don was a healthy, happy baby who grew to be a very inquisitive young man. However, school was not one of his favorite activities. As a boy, he much preferred to play along the river bank and go fishing rather than go to school. After a few days of playing hookey, his school absence was brought to his parents' attention. Receiving a proper reprimand of "You'll not go anywhere but school and bed, young man," he learned that water time after school was better than no water time at all. Thus, scheduling his water time after school hours and when chores were done made it even more enjoyable.

Don always wanted to know how things worked. He lived in a time when electricity was the marvel of the age. New ideas using this power brought many inquiring minds to work. And never one to be idle, Don used his inventive mind to build whatever came to him. By the time he was eleven, he had taken apart the family phonograph and built what was then called a crystal set. It worked, which made it difficult for his parents to punish him. They struck a deal that, in the future, Don would get permission before trying any new projects.

In the spring of 1916, Homer became ill on one of his Pittsburgh trips. When he arrived home on the train, he went straight to bed. The doctor diagnosed Bright's Disease, an inflammation of the kidneys. Within eight months of the diagnosis, Homer was dead at the age of thirty-seven. Nora and Don continued life on their own.

Homer had left a small insurance policy and part ownership in the new Park Theater located on Liberty Street in the middle of town. This theater showed silent films, all the rage at the time, but it gave very little income to Nora. Since this was the day long before Social Security, it was up to Nora to provide for her son in any way that she could. She was a good seamstress, so taking in sewing helped a bit. But they were still renting the house near the river. Bills began to pile up.

Never one to take charity, Nora decided to sell her interest in the Park Theater. This gave her enough to pay bills and invest in a business that she knew rather well, refurbished antiques. She had read books and talked with local merchants as she nurtured a growing interest in all types of furniture.

When she and Homer went to house-keeping, she collected wood and fabric and made her own parlor furniture. It was quite attractive and serviceable.

Now, years later, she took some of the remaining money from the sale and invested it in a few pieces of furniture, six old chairs and a dining table to be exact. With the help of a neighbor who dabbled in furniture fixing, she refinished the items and sold them for a fair profit. That started her business. For the next forty years she traveled the area, buying, repairing, and selling antiques. It paid the rent, put food on the table, and earned her the reputation of being the first antique dealer between Pittsburgh and Erie, Pennsylvania, to sell refurbished antiques.

Don continued following his inventive spirit. During his high school years, he helped supplement the family income by repairing radios. He continued the repair shop in a small shed in the back yard after his high school graduation in 1923. If there had been a college program to capture his interest in radios, he would have gone. Instead he went to work for a local mechanic and pursued his repair business in the evenings and weekends.

Garage mechanic was not to his liking, so he took a job as a baggage handler at the local train depot. This lasted two years until he had saved enough money to open his own radio shop on Thirteenth Street near Liberty Street, the main thoroughfare in town. As radios were all the rage, his business boomed.

Don loved to tinker with radios and speakers, experimenting with modulation and improving his customers' radios as he repaired whatever else may have been the problem that brought them to him. Word of mouth helped his business to grow over the years. The business also gave him time to go fishing, which continued to be his first love.

Nora's interests expanded to include interior decorating and design. As her antique business grew, she was able to hire laborers to do the refurbishing. This gave the time and funds to buy old houses, fix them up and sell them for a profit. At the time, Franklin had an abundance of large old homes that were in dire need of repair.

CHAPTER 2

Thanks to the Oil Boom

BACK IN THE MID nineteenth century, General Charles Miller, a local businessman, profited from the oil boom in the region, thanks to the Drake Well discovery near Titusville, about twenty miles north of Franklin. For years General Miller built many large homes for his employees in and around the town. A cluster of them were built in an area that became known as Miller Park. However, by the late nineteen twenties, with the depression coming on, most of these homes had been abandoned. People just could not afford to live in them, let alone own them, or take care of them.

During this time, Don's radio business was holding its own. His radio sales had tumbled somewhat, but the repair business was steady. Many people would gather around one radio and listen to help them forget their troubles. There were times when radios were repaired for free, so to speak, or paid for as the pennies came in. He didn't mind as long as he could pay the store rent and help his mom keep a roof over their heads. A few fish from a nearby stream always added to the family table.

Nora's business picked up as she began to buy these old homes, remodel them into several apartments, and rent them out for smaller rents that many people could then afford. When she would find herself in need of funds, she would sell a house to one of the few wealthy businessmen in the area. Then she would use the money to invest in her own business.

In the early thirties, General Miller's sons approached Nora about remodeling a few of their large houses in Miller Park into apartments. Since the depression had even hit their own fortunes, they offered her a deal. In partial payment for her remodeling services, they would let her live in the carriage house next to the largest house she would be working on, their father's home in Miller Park. The deal was to let her live there for up to three years rent free. The idea was that within that time the economy just had to get better. She agreed to the deal. Then both she and Don moved into the carriage house.

Now this carriage house was not a cottage, although that is what most people called it, the Miller Cottage. It was two floors with large rooms, high ceilings and three bedrooms. It was surrounded by flower gardens which unfortunately had been left to overgrow and become quite messy. But along with their many talents, both Nora and Don loved gardening. Within a year after moving in, they brought beautiful flowers and shrubs back to life and had a thriving vegetable garden in the small back yard.

CHAPTER 3

And Then There Was Love

ALONG AROUND 1937, LOVE came knocking on Don's door. He met a young woman named Helen Kiskadden. The story was never explained as to how they met. But they both enjoyed a drink now and then after work, so the thought is that they met in one of the local bars. One thing lead to another. On June 21 they ran off to a small town over the state line in New York and were married. Mom did say that they spent their honeymoon camping on a mountain near a place called Driftwood, Pennsylvania. And of course, they even did some fishing.

They lived with Nora in the Miller Cottage. Helen worked at the local phone company. Don's radio business continued to thrive. Nora's business grew as well. Then in November of 1939, my sister, Judy, was born. She was a very healthy baby with a full head of hair. By the time she was three, her hair was bright red, just like her mom's hair. Speaking of hair, Don's had always been brown like his parents, until his mid-thirties when it started to turn gray. He was forty-four when I was born. By then it was almost white. But he was such a handsome man, it looked good on him.

By the late thirties, business improved to the point that Don decided to get his mother into her own home. One day he said to Nora, "How would you like to live in the first house where you and dad set up housekeeping? It's for sale, and I want to buy it for you." Thus, Nora moved into her own home at 801 Buffalo Street in Franklin.

The house was quite large, two stories tall. It set back from the street up on a hill. Nora had the exterior painted gray and trimmed in white. (A note, as of 2022, the house is still there at 801 Buffalo Street, although at last viewing it had been painted a beautiful red.) She then went to work redesigning the interior making two apartments. She lived downstairs on the first floor and rented the one on the second floor. The rooms were large with high ceilings. In her apartment she displayed many of the refurbished antiques that she would sell to local customers. With her income, she started to pay into this new thing called Social Security. It did help her with some income in her later years. Nora lived to the ripe old age of ninety-six.

CHAPTER 4

A New Home

ONE DAY IN 1940, Nora took Don aside and said, "Helen needs her own house." Now Helen had never complained, but Nora could tell that she was ready to have a home of her own. Don had never thought about it one way or another. Then Nora said, "I have $1,200 saved for you from the Park Theater sale. You take it and build a home for your family." So, he did.

Just south of town on a little road called Pone Lane, Don bought about a half an acre of land from a farmer named Gertrude Lake. She owned and worked a large farm along the road with her sons, Red and Denton. I never did know Red's real name, and his hair was red and gray when I knew him as a kid. But I did play with his sons, Bobby and Gary, in my younger days. However, again I digress.

Don built a Cape Cod style house with a small, one car garage set back on the left side of the house. The house had a large kitchen, a living room, a bathroom, and four small bedrooms, two downstairs and two upstairs. It had a full basement with a large coal furnace. One of the two front basement windows was used as an opening with which to fill the coal bin below it. There was also a large metal sink opposite the stairway that was used for a multitude of chores.

Don planted a row of pine trees in a line to mark the right side of the property. There were larch, scotch pine, cedar, and various types of spruce. Across the front yard he planted a row of blueberry bushes near the road. In the backyard near the pines he planted fruit trees—apples, pears, peaches, and plums. Along the back-property line, he built a chicken coop where he raised chickens for eggs and meat. His large vegetable garden comprised the left back corner of the property. He planted a row of raspberry and blackberry bushes between the garden and the chicken coop. Along the left side of the garden, he planted black raspberry bushes and elderberry bushes. Near the back porch he built a rectangular frame about six feet tall. At each post he planted grape vines. Over the years the vines grew to cover the frame with red, white and blue grapes. This small half-acre produced bountiful harvests each year and made a comfortable home for his family.

CHAPTER 5

And Then Came TV

IN THE FORTIES, DON became interested in another new idea, television. Always thinking ahead, Don delved into television with the enthusiasm he had done with radios. As the war ended, the economy did rebound which peaked interest in this new television idea. And of course, he always spent part of his days fishing whenever the weather and the seasons allowed. After all, the main reason to work for oneself is to be able to go fishing when one "got the itch".

As time moved into the fifties, more and more people wanted televisions in their homes. Don sold more and more televisions and antennas. Always one to stay ahead of the market, in 1951, he got an idea to build a television cable system to bring stronger signal to people in Franklin. With the financial help of three area businessmen, he built a large antenna system on the top of a hill just outside of town. He set poles and ran television cable throughout the town. His cable company, known as the Coaxial Cable Company, offered four television channels to his cable customers, three out of Pittsburgh and one out of Erie, Pennsylvania. The three channels out of Pittsburgh were CBS, NBC, and ABC affiliates. The one out of Erie was an NBC affiliate. However, being in a different market, the Erie channel did offer some new programs to the Franklin area.

Helen was the secretary of the company. She kept the records and sent bills out each month. By the mid-fifties people were paying $3.95 per month to receive their television cable service in their homes. Eventually, the company out grew its storefront on Thirteenth Street.

More room was needed, so Don purchased a lot on Route Eight south of Franklin near his home on Pone Lane. Here he built a nice, cement block building. In keeping with his desire to mark his property line, Don planted pine trees along the back of his property. (A note, as of 2022, those trees are still there growing tall and beautiful even though the cement block building has long since gone.)

With the new building, Don had established a separate company from the one in town. This new company was known as the Don Blair Television Company or "dbtv". (One note here—Don always used the small letters "db" in his business logo because, along with his initials, they also referred to the term decibel, a measurement of sound.) The front of the building contained many new televisions on his display floor. He sold DuMont televisions, which were very popular at the time. He continued to sell antennas for those people who lived outside the cable area. But the cable idea was very popular. By the end of the fifties, he had expanded his cable company to include small hamlets around Franklin, such as Utica, Sugar Creek, Dempseytown, and Reno.

Along with televisions, Don continued to sell radios and stereo record players. I remember once, as a child, Dad said, "Hey, Sis, hold out your hand." In my hand he placed a very small, black thing. He said, "Now that is a transistor. It is used in those little transistor radios. But someday, because of this, you will be able to hold a TV in the palm of your hand." And you know, he was right. The transistor was the forerunner of the microchip. Where would we be today without our cell phones.

Shortly after building the home on Pone Lane, Don built a workshop attached to the right side of the garage. Here he spent time doing what he liked second best—tying flies for fishing. You see, Don really was a fisherman at heart. His business was built with the idea that he could always close up and go fishing when the "itch was too much to bear".

CHAPTER 6

You Can Write That Up

WHEN ONE COULD NOT go fishing, one could always think about going fishing or read about going fishing. In 1931 a new magazine came out called "The Pennsylvania Angler Magazine". Don subscribed to this magazine and became friends with the editor, Mr. Alex P. Sweigart.

One day, after a long conversation with Alex regarding good fishing spots in western Pennsylvania, Alex said, "Don, why don't you write that up for the Angler?" Don replied, "Me? Write that up?" "Yes, you. You could write an article about that stream because you know it. Send it to me next week." That's how Alex got Don to write for the Pennsylvania Angler Magazine.

For the next twenty years, he wrote fishing articles for the Angler. The following chapters contain these articles that were written more than seventy years ago. They tell about a time when fishing was more than just a line in the water. It was a special way of life. Maybe it still is. . .

CHAPTER 7

Big Sandy Creek

SOME TIME AGO I suggested to Mr. Sweigart that it would be nice to read each month a description of some Pennsylvania fishing water. To learn from some fellow who lived there the kind, size and quantity of fish I might catch (if they bite) and the tackle generally used. Whether bait was obtainable and what kind, and should I haul the car-top boat a hundred miles or bring a pair of boots?

The Editor wrote immediately in reply, and, before I had read his last paragraph, I knew I had literally stuck my neck out once again. So, I got to work wading up and down Big Sandy and its principle tributaries, South and Little Sandy. I fished and I talked to fishermen. I talked to herons and kingfishers and beavers and before I finished, I was talking to myself something like this:

"Why, here is a creek I thought I knew. I've fished it all my life, but I didn't know one-tenth of it. Look how it goes from west to east. It begins in nearly flat country up near Sheakleyville, meanders along through clay banks and pond weeds, comes down through the town of Sandy Lake looking like a trout brook. Then it widens out again in more weedy flats for several miles. Above Raymilton she plunges into the hills and on to Polk. Here comes Little Sandy with clear spring water and a half-mile below South Sandy with more of the same. About two miles further the creek dips under the viaduct at Pecan on Route 8 and on its rocky way to the Allegheny three miles below. But who ever heard of a stream flowing out of flat country into the hills (some people call them mountains). Mind you, I don't say it runs uphill, but it is peculiar."

Now look at the fish in it. Most every kind native to Pennsylvania can be found along these waters, the largest perhaps being the carp in the quiet waters of the upper creek. I am personally acquainted with several old residenters over three feet in length. Next in size and weight comes a brightly colored Great Northern Pike of which specimens as long as forty inches have been reported, although I have never seen one over thirty, and he, or more likely she, got away.

Smallmouths inhabit the whole creek and largemouths may be found in the upper weedy sections. Perch and sunnies are present and, in the clear waters below Polk, brown, rainbow and a rare brook trout may be found. Both black and red-tailed suckers run the creek to spawn in great numbers each spring, evidently wintering in the Allegheny. Bullheads and several kinds of minnows pretty well complete the list of catchable fishes.

If you are a trout fisherman, you will like South Sandy which bisects State Game Lands No. 39 and is woodland for six or seven miles. Likewise, if you are a fly fisherman, you will get plenty sore at Little Sandy for it runs through farmland and is overhung with alders most all the way.

Remember that most of this water is accessible and therefore well supplied with fishermen throughout the season. However, the Fish Commission seems to be aware of this and is able to maintain the fish population in good shape.

Nymphs and flies of nearly all types abound in these waters, but I found this season that a very few patterns were needed, as follows: first, an Adams No. 14 tied spentwing took brown trout consistently from 10:00 AM the first morning until the middle of May. Then a large drake fly came on to the water, nameless to me, which I hastened to imitate as follows: hook No. 10, cream colored wool body, dark brown or chocolate colored hackle with long narrow wings of mallard breast feathers and a few long strands of the same for a tail. This fly rewarded me generously until I switched to one of the same size and shape but of a yellowish-brown body and lighter almost ginger hackle. This latter fly hatched consistently throughout the latter part of June, July and August, furnishing food for both fishes and countless small birds along the creek who make a great game of catching them. Last evening, plugging for pike between Sandy Lake and Raymilton, I noticed these flies still coming up and perch and bass were taking them, this happening on September 24.

When it comes to tackle for the later season fishing, everything goes. I've seen anything from a fourteen-foot cane pole to the tiny seven-foot Thomas that Howard Hough was reckless enough to let me use one Sunday afternoon. But the standard bait-casting rig predominates and seems to me to be the most practical outfit for both bait fishing and plugging. My own preference is for a very light five-foot bamboo rod, a ten-pound nylon line with four-foot nylon leader and one-fourth ounce lures. I have landed a good many pike on this rig and have yet to have one cut or fray the nylon with his teeth. But maybe you would rather use a wire leader. And if you do, it is all right with me.

You won't need a boat, you can find plenty of places to step in over your boots, and if you do wade the upper end of Big Sandy, don't get stuck in the mud.

About live bait, the great majority of fishing is done with worms and dough-balls. However, occasionally, you will see a minnow fisherman or some hardy fellow who had the ambition to catch a basket of soft crabs in the Allegheny and transport them to the creek. So far as I know, no bait is for sale anywhere along the creek.

Oh yes, there are poisonous snakes, though I have not seen one for several years. There are also poison ivy, mosquitoes and deer flies. Have a good time.

CHAPTER 8

Notes on Pond and Fish

NOTE: THE VIEWS EXPRESSED herein are not meant to conflict with those of any recognized conservation agency. They are set forth here simply with the hope that they may help to add to the total of knowledge concerning fish and fishing.

We have been reading lately considerably on the subject of farm fish ponds. If we recall, the sum of the expert opinion seems to be that the water need be continually sterilized the same as farm fields to assure continuous productivity. Also, that the favored species of fish be bream, to eat the bugs, and big-mouth bass to eat the bream. Now, if we just add a boy to catch the bass that eat the bream that eat the bugs, we have a very nice picture, one well worth some pleasant and/or serious thinking.

In view of the ever-increasing number of Pennsylvania fishermen, such small ponds come up for serious attention. Meaning that the average angler with a Sunday holiday nowadays has a pretty hard time to find peace and solitude along the water.

For one thing, a small spring will provide water for a one- or two-acre pond. There are literally thousands of places in Pennsylvania where small ponds could be made. Further, a small spring is much less liable to future pollution than a large creek or river.

All this has been merely leading up to description of two forty-year-old ponds, from which we have drawn a great deal of pleasure over the years, along with some small knowledge of the habits of the wild creatures who live in and near them. In line with the discussion about farm fish-ponds, these two, after forty years, should be a great deal of help in answering such questions as: (1) is the expense of creating such a pond justifiable in the light of a long investment, or only as a short-term proposition? If neglected, will such water continue to produce fish in usable amounts? Can you catch too many fish from a pond, as by public fishing, so that it must be periodically restocked? How deep must a pond be in northern Pennsylvania? Would there be any other benefits from such a pond beyond those of fish and fishing?

Without attempts to answer each one of these questions individually, let us get along with our pond fishing and let the answers fall in along the way.

Along in 1905 or 1906 they built a new railroad and, in doing so, changed the courses of two warm water creeks. To make the track as straight as possible they cut off, in each case, a bend in the creek isolating a small pond of approximately an acre. Fortunately, in each pond there was a spring to maintain the water level, though we can imagine they got pretty low in those first few years. At any rate, there were the ponds, accidently man-made and there they have stood for all of these nearly forty years. Both ponds are off the beaten path, being in each instance nearly two miles from the nearest highway. In deference to the men and boys who fish in one of these ponds, we shall not give their location further than to say that they are both in the northern part of Pennsylvania.

The one, let's call it the East Pond, is fished quite steadily throughout the summer. The second, we can call it the West Pond, is not fished at all, except by us, so far as we have been able to observe. This makes for a very interesting comparison, when we think about it, a comparison that brings out some unsuspected answers that bear on conservation.

To return to the beginning, both the streams from whence came the ponds, were and still are primarily small-mouth bass waters with minnows, chubs and suckers. And yet neither pond at this time harbors these species. The ponds now contain only big-mouth bass, bream or sunfish and bullheads. How these fish got there is a question we cannot answer except that there must have been a few of each present when the ponds were made. It is hardly likely that they were ever stocked. We notice that these kinds of fish able to stand the high summer temperatures and low oxygen supplies that must have occurred in drought years. The small-mouth, who certainly must have been the predominant predator in the beginning, lost out completely and some time before 1915. For that was when we first became interested. We now feel that the shallow water in these ponds doomed the small-mouths, for we have since many times found the two bass sharing and thriving in the same conditions of water, food, and cover, excepting only that deeper water was available. It is a well-known fact that, in late fall, small-mouth fishermen haunt the deepest holes in the stream. At any rate, after nearly forty years, these two ponds, containing in the beginning practically every kind of stream fish, now hold only big-mouth bass, bream and bullheads.

We are pretty sure that these streams contained carp at the time the ponds were made. If they did, this is the first instance, to our knowledge, in which they failed to survive. And that in itself might bungle up a lot of otherwise logical answers to conservation questions.

Now, at the present time, both ponds contain an adequate supply of big-mouth bass, ranging in weight up to an estimated six pounds. Both ponds have yielded to us, upon occasion, four-pound bass. But right there their similarity begins to fade. On the East Pond, almost any summer evening you can watch the small bass jumping for damsel flies. And, if you are adept with a bass bug, you may hook two or three nice bass about sundown. Most of the men and boys who fish here use large surface plugs or live minnows, and we submit that their bass run larger than the ones we usually hook with bugs or dry flies. But we get a lot more strikes and fun and once in while a fish too large for our light tackle. A long time ago we put our own size limit on these bass, fourteen inches, and have not ever had an occasion to regret it. They are very good to eat.

On the West Pond we rarely see surface activity nor do we ever catch many fish. Remember that this is the virgin water, the pond that nobody but the author ever fishes! Once in a long time here, by our records, about once in three trips we get a strike from a big bass, very rarely a small one. But in all the times we have fished here, we have never been able to kill more than one bass in any one day in the West Pond. And oftener than we got a bass we got a goose-egg, and we have fished there a great many times in the last thirty years for we know the bass are there; dozens of beautiful big, fat, beautiful green and gold big-mouth bass. There is only one reason they won't strike. They just are not hungry. This virgin pond abounds in sunfish. In one afternoon, we caught and released about forty of them. The largest was hardly six inches in over-all length. They all have the oversized head and slender body that indicate under-fed fish. Stunted growth, if you prefer.

Back in the East Pond there are not nearly so many sunfish, but they grow larger, fatter and make a worthwhile prize for a boy to carry home. Here a significant note creeps in. Along in early September we notice that the season's crop of bass will be the same size in both ponds, a sturdy two or three inches. But the bluegills in the East Pond have grown to the size of a half-dollar while those in the West Pond are hardly half as big. We doubt very much if the baby bass eat the baby sunfish at this stage. It is our opinion that the small bass are competing with the sunfish for insect food at this season and that the bass, being far more aggressive and quicker to attack, get all the food they want. If a shortage develops, as it evidently does in the West Pond, it is the sunfish who go hungry. Certainly, we know through these many years that the bass grow big and fat in both ponds. Though one thing we do not know is what finally becomes of the big bass in the West Pond. All we can be sure of is that man does not catch them.

As for the bullheads, in the East Pond they are relatively scarce. We rarely see one under ten inches in length and some are maybe fifteen inches. Here again, as with the sunfish, it looks as if the fast growing aggressive, hungry bass keep the small fry pretty well cleaned up; while the fishing activities of man and boy hold the adult population below the point where they can multiply faster than the bass can eat. Again, as with the sunfish, in the West Pond there are literally hundreds of bullheads, from the small fry that look, in their schools, like little black clouds; up to the largest which will be a slim nine or ten inches. These seem always to be on the lookout for something to eat and are never too hard to catch. We simply manipulate a wet fly where Mr. Bullhead can see it, and he will nearly always open his big mouth and suck it in. When he closes his mouth again, you can set the hook. It is slow work and awfully hard on flies, particularly nerve-wracking if you have been trout-fishing only a short time before.

Twenty years, even ten years ago, the West Pond contained a great number of frogs. We ate a lot of them, but the supply never seemed to suffer from our shooting. Lately they are scarce and small though there has been little hunting for four or five years. This, we think, is because many more large birds (herons and ducks) fish here than did a generation ago.

Both ponds contain turtles of a size to amaze you. Several times during the last three decades we have watched these amphibians at their love-making. Clumsy and slightly ridiculous, they make you wonder about those huge reptiles who inhabited this earth so many millions of years in the past.

Nowadays, snapping turtles seem to be universally condemned as predatory creatures; creatures that should be destroyed. After these years of association with these two ponds, we feel that this is unjust, if not entirely wrong. Certainly, the case of the West Pond, with its greatly overstocked numbers of sunfish and bullheads, is proof that the turtles are not damaging to the supply of fish. And there are quite a few turtles, many, many more than you would find in a pond frequented by people with .22's.

Since a turtle in captivity will eat almost anything classed as edible, it seems logical to assume that he will not be overly particular in the wild.

Water snakes have never been numerous in either pond, even in those days before the birds came back. We have long held a suspicion that the turtles were responsible for their scarcity. Along this line of thinking there is a small pond located just outside the city limits here which literally crawls with water snakes. The bottom of this small pond is paved with broken bottles and tin cans, mute evidence that every boy with a new .22 or B.B. gun hikes over there to test his marksmanship. There are no turtles, which we suppose is in support of the boys good shooting. Seems reasonable to think that continuous plinking could exterminate the turtles and that it would be impossible for the boys to kill all the snakes. But in the ponds where the turtles remained undisturbed the snake population never grew out of bounds in all these nearly forty years.

All this observing, then, has led us to the conclusion that the turtle's role in the pond is principally one of scavenger, to clean up the dead, wounded or diseased creatures; and that in some way unknown to us his presence keeps the snake population down to within reasonable numbers. We propose, therefore, that the turtle is a necessary addition to the pond.

As regards fertilizing, we can pretty safely assume that neither pond has ever seen even a handful of commercial fertilizer in all the years. Both ponds are located, of course, in wild land, second growth timber stands on the surrounding hills in sufficient density to prevent surface erosion. Thus, the ponds did not choke with mud and silt which they would certainly have done if less fortunately situated. Very little surface water drains into either pond. This, we believe, is very important for the time and labor necessary to build such a pond would be soon wasted if silt were permitted to enter. Evidently whatever fertilizer is present in these two ponds comes either from the spring water or is manufactured on the spot by the action of the summer sun on the existing plant life in and near the water. Since the East Pond is fished quite a bit and the fish maintain a good rate of growth it would certainly indicate that commercial fertilizers are not an absolute necessity. The simple fact that these men and boys are willing to hike several miles is proof that the fishing remains good. And there is plenty of fishing water in the vicinity that is accessible without so much walking.

In line with this discussion of fertilizing, a colony of beavers provided an interesting experiment on the West Pond several years ago. When they moved in, they naturally decided that the pond was not big enough. The dam they built raised the water level perhaps eighteen inches and flooded a flat strip of land alongside the original pond. Now this land was definitely on the barren side, unproductive. The beavers, after maintaining the water level for two seasons, either left or were trapped out and the pond then returned to its original level. That spring sprang up the most luxurious crop of weeds and grasses we have ever seen anywhere. And the rank growth continues yet, though not so wildly as it did that first year. Something in that pond water unlocked the door to vigorous growth. What it was we do not pretend to know. But, by the process of elimination, we can hazard the guess that it was that action of the summer sun upon the shallow water and the minute plants and animals suspended in it. Thanks anyhow to the beavers for performing the experiment.

If there is any basis of fact in all of this, it bears out one thing, that a considerable depth of water is not needed for these kinds of fish. Since neither pond under discussion has a high-water depth exceeding four feet and in periods of extreme drought little more than half of that, it follows that the expense of building dams of eight or ten or more feet is hardly necessary in this climate. Limiting the depth of future manmade ponds to this four foot maximum might also prevent tragedy from overtaking some of the many boys who would no doubt put to sea upon them in small home-made boats or unreliable rafts. So, since through these nearly forty years, these fish in these two ponds have survived and prospered in the face of our sometimes very severe northern Pennsylvania winters and summer droughts, we can pretty safely conclude that the depth of four feet is adequate and that greater depth would serve no useful purpose.

The doe who came unafraid one evening to wade and drink and the two magnificent bucks with their huge horns in the velvet, of which they are so careful, the blue jay who warned them of my presence and the young blue heron who made his home on the West Pond this past summer; these we have seen and enjoyed. The family of flying squirrels who live in a hollow tree trunk, surrounded by water like a medieval castle, have held us breathless with their graceful diving and gliding as they trade between their castle home and a hemlock on the shore. And the old woodchuck, who trusts me now, coming along the bank one spring day with a round peck of dry oak leaves in his teeth, each one held carefully by the stem. And those amazing little diving ducks, who can submerge like submarines, and reappear without making the tiniest ripple on the surface of the evening pond. These and many more are the extra dividends these two ponds have given us, and, if our scientific data is not as exact as it might have been, it is simply because of these many absorbing distractions. Sometimes we even got to fish.

In summing up all our pleasant hours spent along the ponds, one thing stands out clearly, that is that panfish must constantly be caught out or bass fishing will not be good. Thus, it would seem wise to locate such ponds where they would be accessible to the younger fishermen.

And in conclusion, forty years is just a tiny moment in the greater scheme of things; but it is the greater part of a man's active life. Now that we know that a wisely placed little pond will last so long, our advice to any young man who lives on the land or who intends to return to it when peace comes again is build yourself a pond, it will bring you peace and recreation as long as you live.

CHAPTER 9

The Little Frogs

GOING FISHING. THE FORD and I ambled carefully down a puddly back-woods road that September afternoon. It was wet, and the air was clean and spring smelling. The early morning thunderstorm had cleansed not only the air but had washed with gentle thoroughness each leaf and twig and blade of grass. I hoped that the warm water from the sky had tempered the creek so the bass would be on that last savage feeding splurge before they left for the winter quarters. What a pleasant life they led; to live under the summer sun, and sleep away the bitter months.

But a treacherous looking puddle aroused me, and as the car and I approached, judging, we saw a dozen little frogs sitting all around it. Serenely quiet, that was their habit. When the car was near enough, they jumped, raggedly, hurriedly; but amazing thing, they jumped not into the water to hide as frogs should, but scrambled into the weeds along-side and away from the road. How had they learned that a car would smash them if they hid in the water? They were only a few weeks old. Why had they not been killed when the first car came along? What would they do if a man walked down the road instead of a car? That I found out, for I drove on a ways, parked the car, and, waiting, walked back toward the puddle. They did. When I got close enough, they all jumped in the water! So, I went fishing.

When I had a chance, I took down Darwin's books and had read a lot of interesting things before it occurred to me; shucks, there were no automobiles running up and down those back-woods roads when he wrote those books. This is one thing I will have to follow through alone. Natural selection had nothing to do with these little frogs that I could see. Their mammas had probably never seen a car, for the road had only been built this last winter to serve a lumber camp. That was when they were but tadpoles, swimming around the shallow water, under the ice, wondering. That is about all tadpoles seem to do.

But here were the little frogs, facing a new danger that uncounted generations of ancestors had never experienced, and surviving because their tiny brains triumphed over instinct. Slowly, that September afternoon, the ideas began to come clear in my own mind. If these little frogs could be so smart, so young; why could not the game fishes learn to outwit man's devices for capturing them? Why couldn't they live and grow and prosper in hard fished water just as well as in primitive places. If those six weeks' old frogs could think for themselves and avoid death, why not a brown trout whose ancestors had faced thousands of artificial flies since Izaac's time? Did a bass, who struck a plug one night and luckily escaped, come back to grab another the next night or did the lesson stay with him? Did the fishes learn to recognize a fishing line for the danger signal that it is? The creek was low and the water clear as glass that sunny afternoon. It was the perfect place to begin my experiments.

My tackle was new and I was young and eager. Now neither of us, the split-bamboo or I, are as swiftly resilient as we were that day. The rod served me well for many years, until one day—but that is a later story. As I waded, dished and watched along that newly opened stretch of back-woods creek and saw the bass loafing in the shallow eddies; saw some of them rush twenty or fifty feet to hit that shiny plug bedecked with vicious gang hooks, I wondered if they would be there five or ten or twenty years later. Would they be as eager to strike these crazy gadgets after they or their fathers had tasted them? Would they be capable of learning to avoid man and his fishing tackle and could they somehow pass the knowledge on to their children?

Many more than twenty years have passed by, and swiftly, too, and everything is changed. That most hopeful species of man, the fishermen, have multiplied by leaps and bounds. On any pleasant Sunday you can see them by the dozens, milling up and down, enjoying the quest; but rarely the conquest, of the fish the creek contains. The creek and the bass have not multiplied apace with the fishermen. The water flows in about the same volume. It is, luckily, still pure, clear and clean. True, the tangled tree-tops left by the loggers have rotted away, and a new forest has grown up, but the willows along the banks still fight their yearly battle with the winter's ice and the pools and eddies have changed but little. The adjacent highway has changed from a rutted wagon track to a broad paved speedway and, in the hollow by the bridge, the stench of burned gasoline hangs blue and heavy on an August afternoon. Well trampled paths lead up and down the creek's banks, pointing out every favored pool and eddy. Charlie calls it a "Sunday best" creek. What he means is; you could fish along its banks via the well-trampled paths with little fear of snagging or soiling your newest Sunday go-to-meeting clothes.

So much for the fishing water and the multiplying fishermen. What once was virgin woods and water is now a thoroughly trampled recreation ground, complete with broken glass and scattered paper. It has come about far more quickly than I ever dreamed it would, that September afternoon long ago. If it could happen here, won't it eventually happen everywhere? And, although man's ability to travel hither and yon has grown so tremendously in the years past, certainly it is going to double and redouble in the future. Look forward then, with me, to the time when no remote Canadian lake or Alaskan river will be without its quota of fishermen; when the time comes when there is no more virgin fishing water to explore; and you make up your mind that you might as well fish in your own home creek as roam the world. But it is not a condition to be afraid of, like the loss of a friend; but something we should accept and study so that we can pass on to our children, and they to theirs some, if not all, the joys and thrills we have experienced in fishing. And I do not mean that we should sit like fogies and tell tall tales of the past. Imaginative creatures that we fishermen are, in one or two generations—wow!

Because I had an inkling of what was coming and because the behavior of those little frogs caught in my imagination, I stayed at home and fished. I sought to enumerate that bass in my creek and when I caught them, I returned to the water all that were unhurt. As the years rolled by and the fishermen became more numerous, I became better and better acquainted with the creek and the bass. As I watched and fished, some years the bass would be very scarce and again I thought the creek was fished out as everyone had said; but then in other seasons they would be numerous as ever. This intrigued me for many years. But one fact became plain and solid in my mind as the years rolled by. It was that it took an ever-increasing skill on my part to catch the bass. Many hundreds of times in these later years have I deftly (or accidentally) dropped my plug close by a clump of weeds or a sheltering rock only to see a bass swirl toward and then away from it as he recognized the fraud. I stole along carefully behind the willows so they could not see me and watched them lazing in the sun, unalarmed as the shadow of a kingfisher passed swiftly among them. But when the plug flew high over them the shadow of the line attached sent them racing for the depths. I watched them scurry away as I waded into the creek and then, as I stood motionless, cruise slowly back to examine me. And I never caught one who did that. But I did learn some little tricks to fool them and catch them by. Had I not learned, what a sorry thing my ego would have become if I were forced to admit that I was not a little smarter than the "poor fish". So that is what this is all about; fish do have brains and they can learn to beware the fisherman and his hooks. But they can be caught in hard fished waters, and the feeling of success that comes when the smart ones are caught is much more memorable than that of catching fish where no other fisherman has preceded you.

For some years we maintained a hunting camp in the mountains of central Pennsylvania. It was an abandoned farmstead. At the foot of a huge maple tree down over the bank was a good spring, no longer used, for we had drilled a well by the kitchen. One spring day some of us decided to enlarge the pool and stock it with some native trout. Half-a-dozen men with pick and shovel soon made a pool six by eight feet and nearly three feet deep. Then we adjourned to the stream nearby and caught a dozen small trout and carried them in buckets to the pool. They grew and prospered and became remarkably tame. They ate almost anything, bread and bits of meat, and it was no uncommon sight to see a knot of husky men clad in heavy boots and woolens spading the frozen December earth, hunting worms to feed the trout. But one afternoon in summer, when the trout were mostly eight and ten inches long, we showed some visiting children how they would take a worm from your fingers if you held it quietly in the water. This palled on the kids after a while, and they wanted to do some real fishing. So, we rigged up a rod and line, but instead of using a hook, we simply tied the worm to the end of the string. It worked swell. The trout would grab the worm, run under the bank, and when the kids pulled would come out fighting furiously; until forced to the top of the water where he let go. No harm was done, and we thought nothing of it when the fish quit biting after a while. But the next time we tried it we found out that those fish wanted nothing to do with a worm that had a white string tied to it. Nor did they ever take such a bait again though we did get some to take worms on a black thread and on gut leaders, but never as aggressively as they did that first time. They learned something. So, did we.

I met a rather mature brown trout one day along a tributary to my creek. That was the year I learned that it is better to use a large spent-wing dry-fly for late season trout fishing rather than to putter with long leaders and tiny flies. A trout will come a long way in clear water to take a big fly when he will hardly move a foot to take a tiny one. Much easier and better to have the fish come to your fly than to try to approach too closely on a July day. It was the thrill supreme to see that great trout wallow into the shallow water to take a big floating Queen of the Waters. Not for long though, for as soon as he felt the barb he plunged under these tangled roots and snapped my leader as easily as a bull would break a clothesline. Certainly, he took my breath away, but when I regained it, I climbed that leaning tree to watch for him. In a little while I saw him on the bottom, rolling on his side, rubbing that fly against the rocks. He got it out and presently resumed his feeding, but no matter what I offered I could not get another rise out of him. He would come and examine everything, but when he saw the leader or the hook, he turned away. Finally, in desperation I caught some grasshoppers and tossed them on the water. He ate every one but the one with the hook in it. I never did catch him, and I doubt if anyone did for, he was plenty big enough to have had his name in the papers. I think that he knew about hooks and lines when he struck the first time, but that he was in too much of a hurry to grab that fly and get back, to examine it carefully.

Several warm-water streams we know that would normally be fished by boys looking for sunnies or suckers have been classed as trout streams by the authorities and get an annual restocking of legal-sized brown or rainbow trout. Most of the trout are promptly caught out by the fellows who get there on Opening Day. A few remain, but the amazing thing is the number of bass who survive the torrent of flies and spinners, worms and minnows that descend upon the waters each spring. The time to count the bass is, of course, later when the water is low and clear. This does not mean that bass are smarter than trout. It just goes to show that, having been educated in the ways of men and hooks and lines, the bass disdain from biting, where the trout, lacking that education, are caught.

Several times I have seen the results of accidental poisoning of fishing water. The latest and most vivid being that of what I can honestly describe as one of the hardest fished eddies in the country. This pool continued to produce an occasional nice fish; plenty to encourage the hopes of the neighborhood fishermen. When the sudden poisoning came, we were all astounded at the size and numbers of the game fish killed, which had till then avoided capture by hook and line. Some were bigger than any we had ever caught.

The future, then, with its ever-increasing number of fishermen, need not frighten anyone. My little creek has proved that given pure and fertile water, food and cover, the fish will carry on. And, though the fishermen try as they will, they can never exterminate the bass in my creek, so long as they fish with hook and line bait or plug or fly. The main point is to continue the fight against pollution wherever and however we can. Here, too, the future looks brighter than the past. If there is strength in numbers, we are, or mighty soon will be, strong enough to rise and say that these streams are to be ours to fish in and not to be despoiled for any other purpose.

The tricks to use to catch these educated bass? We will discuss those and soon, but right now we are going fishing.

CHAPTER 10

Bait Casting

THERE IS A CERTAIN mechanical contrivance, usually built into a stout box with a lever on the side. Pretty lithographs of bright lemons and some other fruit whirl about whenever a coin is inserted and the lever yanked. It carries a peculiar fascination for many American people. Once in a long time something happens to the cogs inside, and it belches a cupful of coins which are known collectively as the Jackpot. Oh, happy day! But, since the little cogs move in their own mysterious ways to perform their rare miracles, few people have ever become financially independent by their whims. Tussling with the lever provides a certain amount of exercise and, too, each yank carries with it a sort of forlorn hope that this is the one that will finally bring success. How like bait-casting for fresh-water game fish. The cast, the whirling cogs, the forlorn hope that goes out each time and returns, dwindling. Then, when you least expect it, the jolting strike, the breathless battle, and success.

Lady Luck can be a hard task-mistress as well as a generous one. She will reward the just or the unjust, the amateur or the expert, with equal carelessness. In an old dictionary, under "fisherman" I saw this definition; "one who catches fish." The up-to-date word-pond has this to offer: "one who fishes," it says nothing about his ability or his luck. So, I say, if you would catch fish by casting plugs and spinners at them, cultivate Lady Luck. With her by your side you are bound to be successful, without her you are doomed. How to invoke the mistress? Why, any boy can show you how to spit on your bait. Charlie's expression, after I have suffered some especially disastrous bit of bad luck, is: "You don't go to church often enough." And he is probably right.

My fifteen-year-old cousin and I were prowling the creek one day. We came to the deep, dark pool the beavers had made, and spied a fisherman, an old man, sitting on the bank.

"A beautiful day."

"You betcha."

"Any luck?"

"Nothing doing today, I guess."

As we talked, he reeled in to examine his bait. And it was without doubt the biggest run chub I have ever seen. He cast it out again.

"What you fishin' for?"

"Pike." (Esox Lucius)

"He must be a big one."

"He is. I been fishin' for him all summer. But he ain't bit yet."

He turned to the boy whose eyes had bugged when he saw the bait. Running his eye over the light casting rod, the thin line and the tiny plug, he said to him:

"Why don't you give him a try? He lays right by that old stump."

"O. K." said the boy. He stepped forward, dropped the plug to his hand and pointing it at the stump, expectorated neatly through his teeth upon his hand. He grinned, reeled the plug up to the rod-tip, wiped his hand on his breeches, and sent the plug out to drop expertly by the stump. The brown water boiled green and silver. The plug disappeared. That pike looked big around as a stove-pipe. Then the thin line snapped. Nobody said anything. The old man reeled in his big chub, unhooked it, and dropped it into the creek. As he gathered up his tackle he finally spoke.

"Well I guess I can get at my potatoes. He won't bite now for two weeks anyhow."

So, you see it pays to keep Lady Luck always beside you if you can. Like a lot of other girls, she will make things hum when she is around. But you have got to do your part. She won't untangle backlashes or drop your plug expertly by a stump. You can't expect her to climb a tree to retrieve a plug or to fetch the bottle of mosquito-dope you are always forgetting. Her part is to provide the excitement, the drama. Yours it is to do the practicing that makes a skilled caster, to do the observing of the fishes' habits so you will know where, when and what to offer them. So, we had better begin.

Let us assume that you have a good baitcasting rod and reel. It need not be expensive, here in America, to be good. But here I have a tip for you. If it is expensive, you will take good care of it. And it will serve you many times longer than a cheaper one that you neglect. Besides, you will be a better caster if you cherish your equipment. We also assume that you have learned enough about casting to be able to toss a plug fifty or sixty feet with some accuracy. If you have progressed to or passed this stage you will soon come to a fork in the road. One path will lead you into being a caster for casting's sake or the other one will take you down the road to being a fisherman. We will further assume that you turn to the right; that is, you want to catch fish.

To keep first things first, after learning to throw the plug with a little accuracy the next important problem is where to throw it. The first plug I ever saw was about six inches long, and if my little boy memory is correct, it had five gangs of treble hooks. Some of the older fellows had it and during the course of the casting demonstration that ensued, one of them hooked a by-stander squarely in the cheek with it. I, the little boy, stood by and watched Doc cut those hooks out, wash the blood away and cover his face with bandages. I never forgot it. Every fisherman has eyes in the back of his head, or if he has not, he looks.

If the small-mouth bass is to be your favorite quarry you will learn quickest about his habits, his feeding and loafing hang-outs, if you fish along a small clear stream. You will learn, for instance, that no amount of loud talk has any effect on him, but a careless foot against a stone will send him racing. So, you have our permission to swear at the top of your voice when things go wrong. You will learn that plugs coming swiftly downstream faster than the current get more vicious strikes than those being pulled up against the current. You will learn the places where he lies in wait for food, in the weeds, beside a stone or under a cut bank. A quiet spot beside the current or often on the bottom under the current where he can flash up to kill his supper. But, by all means, learn how shy and scared he is when you approach and when you graduate to bigger streams or lakes don't ever forget how few you caught in the little creek after you had scared them. Even where you can't see, he can. Remember that he does most of his hunting at night, like an owl.

After you have caught some fish you will probably buy more plugs and then some more until you end up with a sizable boxful. That is all right. Uncle Sam gets a nice little royalty off each one in the shape of excise tax, and he always needs the money. So be as patriotic as you like. But after a while you will notice that you always pin your hopes on the same two or three every time you fish anyway, so why lug that big box around?

The accuracy of casting is most important, no question about it, but I would far rather have you practice it along the creek than in the back yard. That is the place where you may learn that your plug, dropped squarely into his hiding place, is most likely to provoke an instantaneous strike. But that if it drops three or four feet away, he will only scoot for safety, or at best, eye it with disdain. You will not be a fisherman until you have learned to finish out a cast and start the retrieve with your right hand while you are swatting mosquitoes with your left. Nor can you learn, at home, to make a side-swipe cast in under the low branches of an elm, or a little back-hand cast when you are tangled up in the willows. If you love to fish you will learn these little things without conscious effort. You can learn that a plug landing with a gentle "splat" is much more liable to be struck at than one landing with a loud splash. So, you develop the system of halting the plug in mid-air over your target so it will fall into the water instead of diving in with all the velocity of the cast. That your shadow must never precede you to the water. If the sun is shining in your eyes—OK., but if it is coming over your shoulder—bad. All these things and many more can be learned, and quickly, if you will fish along a small stream where the water is clear, and you can watch the fish. And they will apply not only to the bass but in considerable measure to the other game fishes, the trout, the pike or the muskellunge. You may also learn the all-important secret advantage we bait-casters have over the live-bait fishermen.

One day when I was a young lad I lay on a big rock and watched a half-dozen bass loafing in the clear water. I hooked a soft crawfish to my line and dropped it into the pool whereupon the bass all gathered round, like people at an accident, and watched it sink to the bottom. As it righted itself and started to crawl toward a little stone one of the bass moved in, grabbed it by the scruff and gave it a vicious shake. Then he dropped it, backed up and resumed his place in the circle. They all watched, and when the crawfish showed signs of life another one of the bass moved in and gave it the same treatment, for all the world like a terrier with a rat. This time it was finished and, after they had watched it a few moments, they turned away, bored again. They killed three like that before I got wise and moved on.

One afternoon Forrest and I were floating down the Alleghany. We came upon a fisherman anchored at the head of an eddy.

"How they bitin'"

"Not bitin'."

"What you usin'"

"Crabs and minnies."

"Well, that's a good place, they ought to bite."

"I ain't had a bite all day."

Forrest and I had been casting casually as we drifted along for it was yet early and the eddy we wanted to fish was a mile farther on. Forrest said to the fellow, joking, "I bet there is a bass under your boat."

And he dropped the plug about three feet from the side of his boat, as we drifted past. There was. And he struck. He was a dandy. And he almost jerked Forrest into the river before he woke up. So it is, these game fishes have a lust to kill that makes them strike sometimes even when they are not hungry. The success of some plugs that resemble nothing whatever that a fish might call food helps to bear out these observations. Thus, we have, with our plugs and spoons and spinners, opportunities to catch fish that the live-bait fishermen do not. Their chances are limited to the contents of the fish's stomach; ours include not only his appetite but what may be in his head, as well.

Since you more than likely learned to cast in the copy-book manner, with a book (real or imaginary) under your elbow, and thus mastered the fact that casting is not a matter of main strength but simply of storing energy in the rod on the back-swing and guiding as you release the power in the forward cast, the whole trick began to seem very simple. Once it became clear to you that the easy way was the best way, backlashes were no longer a problem. And that a thin line, ten, twelve, or fifteen pounds casts easier than the heavier ones. You may find, as I have, over a period of a great many years, that you land a better percentage of large fish with a light line than you do with a heavy one! With confidence in a heavy line you fight harder and either pull the hooks out of the fish or enlarge the holes in his flesh so he can get rid of them. Because a thin line is more elastic, it is easier to keep taut during speedy maneuvers. But you must keep those hooks needle sharp.

On the subject of lines, you may sometime experience a spell of discouraging backlashes. Don't be like the poor Indian and chop off that offending thumb. First try another line. Some lines lose their water-proofing and swell or turn sticky so that casting with them is practically impossible. Along the Alleghany water shed nearly all the water has a film of crude oil floating upon it at times. After your line has picked up a little of this, but it is no doubt just as well that you have not heard some of the comment made by strangers here, anent their casting abilities, once their lines have been oiled by this Pennsylvania crude. I can't recall any that would be printable.

By confining, at first, your bait-casting to a small, clear stream you will be able to see how important is the beginning of your retrieve. The instant your be-hooked gadget hits the water, it must begin to get the——out of there or your fish will find out what it is, a lifeless thing for which he has no use or need. As the plug approaches the spot you extend your arm, pointing it and rod at the target, you check the cast with your thumb and begin the retrieve with your thumb on the spool. Bringing the rod back and up with your thumb still in place you may be surprised to discover that you can bring it a good ten feet at whatever speed you please without once touching the reel-handles. Now, keep the rod tip at a good angle to the line as you change hands on the rod to finish reeling in the cast. Please don't ever point your rod at your plug at any time during your retrieve. There are certain long, slender fish that delight in striking your plug just as you lift it from the water. Keep your rod at an angle to the line, let the rod absorb the shock. Believe me, I learned the hard way, broken lines, skinned knuckles; but worst of all, big ones that got away. I have asked a lot of fellows along the river why they pointed their rods this way, at the plugs, and most of them told me, to prevent wearing out their lines. I can buy new lines, but I cannot buy a prize fish.

In the beginning we advised your courting Lady Luck. In summation, we are thoroughly convinced that the best way to catch fish is to have her on your side. A number of years ago Floyd fished with Charlie and I quite a bit for bass. We fished in the afternoons, with crawfish. But he changed jobs and that meant either fishing at night with plugs or on Sundays with us. He had scruples against fishing on Sunday, and Charlie and I respected him for it. We felt, too, that since according to the Book, the fish were here before we were, they should have a Sabbath, if they so desired it. But later we decided that most of the fish loafed most of the time anyhow, and they did not need a day to rest. So, Floyd took up plugging, and without success. He fished, and he caught nothing. We loaned him baits we had caught fish with, and still he caught none. Finally, one night, we went along. We stood in the river, a few yards on either side of him, and caught bass; he never had a strike. Eventually Charlie and I tired of fishing and sat upon a rock, spoiling the clean night air with a lot of flippant advice. Floyd kept dog-gedly at it. So, Charlie said:

"I bet you the best cigar in the store, you don't catch one in the next ten casts."

That did it. Floyd started to reply, but he never had a chance. He was the busiest man you ever saw, fighting his first plug-caught bass. And, once the ice was broken, or Lady Luck had changed her mind, he caught them right along with us. To be quite truthful, as a fisherman ought not to be, he and his luck have beaten us any number of times.

CHAPTER 11

The Magic Spoon

CHARLIE NAMED IT. It surely had an uncanny attraction for warm-water game fish. Not only that, but it hooked them and held them better than any other spoon we ever used. The day he named it, I stopped by his place to see if I could persuade him to go fishing. I anticipated no great argument. He is the sort of fellow who would rather fish than eat, except at meal-time. But he was away ahead of me; with an early lunch under his belt, he had already gone fishing. To find him along the river was no problem; he always worked the same eddy when he was alone. Sure enough, when I arrived, there he was idly casting a floating plug across the shallows. "Just practicing," he said, trying out a new reel.

"I've got a new spoon I made," I said. "Watch how it swims."

"Humph, you and your everlasting spoons, why don't you make something that looks like something a bass would eat."

"Well, you watch, this thing really swims." And I heaved it out across the shallow water in front of him. Bang, it had not traveled ten feet until a bass nailed it.

"Beginner's luck," he chortled as the fish splashed, jumped, and shook his head. I netted it, got the hooks out, and turned it loose. Charlie examined the spoon. "A piece of brass," he said. "With trout hooks on it. He must have been a blind one. A piece of brass with a feather on the end. Why don't you make something pretty once?"

"But watch how it swims, this thing looks alive. And did you see how those hooks were tangled up in his tongue? That means he was really after it. You know how many times you hook 'em on the outside of the face like they had turned away at the last minute, and you just snatched them."

So, I trolled along in front of him, so he could see its action in the water. It wiggled like a tadpole in a hurry.

"It sure is a squirmy thing," he admitted, after watching it. "But it don't look like nothing I would eat."

"Well, you remember we were talking about the carp, and where all the millions of little ones go that are hatched out every year. This is supposed to be the imitation. You know the yellow flash they make when they roll, like this thing does. But I thought gold would be too rich for a blooming carp, so I made it out of brass."

"It does shoot out a yellow light," he admitted softening, but far from convinced. "But I bet you can't catch another bass here with it, right in the middle of the day."

I hardly expected I could, either, but I tried. A hundred yards farther along the river bank I got another strike, smaller. And Charlie melted, "Magic, that's what it is. Brass and carp, he says. I say it's magic."

When I had finished the spoon and started out, I had not intended to fish in the river. I wanted to try out the spoon in the beaver ponds up the creek. There were big pike in the brown water, back there. Smart ones who would roll up and bunt an ordinary lure with their mouths shut or simply follow along behind until you lifted your plug from the water and then splash water in your face as they turned insolently away. I was sore at those pike because I couldn't catch them. Charlie was a bass fisherman; he was disdainful of snakes, as he called them. But I knew if he ever saw a really big one follow his bait he would be as eager to catch him as I had become. I finally persuaded him to come along with me, though he agreed to come more, I think, because the sun was hot and bright along the river than because he thought there was good fishing in prospect. The idea of spending the afternoon in the shade was a powerful argument. So, we went back to my car and up the creek. To properly impress him with the wildness of the beaver ponds, I drove in the wrong road so we had to walk a mile to the creek. I did not tell him we could have driven almost to it by another road. Mean trick, sure. But because he thought he was in a wilderness, he fished them harder. Fortunately, it was a day in mid-week, and we had the water to ourselves.

We came to the creek and the brown water of the beaver ponds from the untrampled side, and it did look like a wild place. Not until Charlie, used to casting on the wide Alleghany, tossed his plug across the creek and snagged it in some roots on the other bank, did he discover that a lot of other people knew about this place and fished in it. He was righteously grumpy about my deception. But before that happened, he had seen some big carp and at least one good bass loafing in the shade on top of the water. So, he kept on plugging. Then one of those old pike splashed water on him. He saw it coming and nearly swallowed his pipe. But of course, the fish never meant to grab his plug, just chase it out of there. And after Charlie got his voice back up in his throat where it belonged, he began to talk about the so-and-so blankety-blank fish scaring you like that when they never intended to strike. Then I advised him to put on another plug and try him again. He will lay right there in front of you for a while, I told him, just to see what you have got to offer. So, he took off the red and white plug and put on a yellow one. Once, twice and three times he cast the plug out and reeled it in and then the same thing happened. Another big swirl, a tail-flipping splash, and the fish disappeared in the dark water. No strike. Charlie's temper was a trifle frayed, as mine had been so many times. Finally, he said:

"Now let's see you work the magic on this baby."

"That's what I made this gadget for," I said. "To see if I could fool him. So, step to one side, please, and watch him commit suicide."

He did not do anything so foolish. I tossed the spoon up along the bank, out a little from the shore, and brought it back over him as fast as I could reel. He lunged at it, mouth wide open like a white cavern, turned as he struck, jumped, and while I tried frantically to tighten up the line, the spoon came straight back at me like a high hard fast one from the pitcher's box. I ducked. Charlie lit his pipe again and spoke.

"You got the magic, alright, but it's a good thing he never learned to throw a curve; he'd have beaned you sure."

So, it was a memorable trip. Between then and sundown, the Magic Spoon caught seven little pike, but none to take home. And Charlie got a 16-in. bass to hit his yellow plug, so his joy was complete. He is nearly always ready to go pike fishing now-a-days, with confidence in the brass gadget with the trout hooks on it.

We figured there were at least three reasons why the new spoon worked. It was something new, different. We noticed for a long time that a new plug comes on the market, is advertised, and catches fish. Everybody buys one, tosses it around, and in the short span of a couple years every bass in the country has bit on it and finished his career in the skillet, or, escaping, has had a lesson in what not to strike. If there is any truth in that statement, and my years of bait casting in civilized waters have convinced me there is, the most successful caster will try to find out which bait is popular with the fishermen, and buy or make something exactly opposite. The Magic Spoon was certainly the opposite of the floating wobblers everybody was casting in those snag-infested beaver ponds.

Secondly, it looked alive as it swam through the water. Squirmed, as Charlie so aptly phrased it. No matter what sort of live thing the fish thought it was, and that we can never know, they could not help but think it was alive, for it really swam. And, third, even if the first big one to hit it threw it at me, it gave a better average of landed fish to strikes than any other spoon we ever used. Spoons, as a rule, hook fewer bass than do plugs simply because they dart about in the water, something like a terrified minnow, but more unpredictably, from the bass's viewpoint. I can't imagine a bass, catching and eating two or three minnows a day, learns about angles and the leading of targets as does a professional skeet shooter. And the bass has more at stake than the shooter, he has to get his target, or he don't eat. But he misses the minnows often when he is slashing at them. Later on, I think I can explain why he misses.

If you are interested, for this spoon has never been placed on the market, here is how I made the first one. I found a thin sheet of brass and cut from it an elongated egg shape, three inches long and an inch wide. I drilled a small hole in each end of it. Then, with a machinist's hammer and a block of soft wood for an anvil, I tapped and tapped until I had it deeply spooned. I bummed a good stout hook from Charlie, for he is not ashamed to fish with live bait, broke the eye off and bent and ground the shank to fit inside the spoon. I plugged the little holes with toothpicks, turned the hook and the inside of the spoon with solder. Then, burning my fingers, I soldered them together, filling the spoon with solder to add weight. Now it looked something like a very popular manufactured spoon except for the hole in the end at the base of the hook. But I was only half finished. I got a few barred feathers from a wood-duck, how, I can't recall. And two No. 6 trout hooks (light weight) and with a loop of wire made a double hook by soldering wire and hooks together. Such double hooks are common today, made from one piece of wire without solder. I tied the wood-duck feathers to the double hook like the wings of a wet fly, upright, and back to back. This was the tail of the Magic Spoon. So, with a little split ring I joined the two parts together. Then, with a file and rod and reel I moved from the workshop to the creek. By filing here and there on the spoon, I finally made it swim. If the tail was too bulky it would kill the action of the spoon. If the spoon was too wide in proportion to its length and weight, it would dart and flop and spin. When every detail came right, it swam, wiggled steadily along, wagging its tail like a happy dog. The spoon foiled up vertically on one side and then the other, flashing, and the flat tail wagged from side to side. Back to the shop we went and polished the brass, and painted the inside solder with a warm yellow. I put a barber pole stripe of red down the spoon for good measure, just the artistic touch.

So, I had a spoon almost as straight running as a spinner, something a bass could hit every time he shot, if he drew his sights fine and sure. A bait that flashed the challenge of food easily, caught, and fit to eat. Charlie called it magic. I remain of the opinion it was a lot of hard but pleasant work. Now maybe someday we can get a factory to make Magic Spoons enough for all of us. Then, in a couple of years, we will have to invent something new again. Though it is always fun to experiment. And who but Americans invent so many gadgets?

Of course, the brass outside needs continual polishing to keep it bright and shiny, like the golden scales of a carp minnow. There are several ways or means to tackle this angle. You could turn the job over to someone else. Or you could carry the quart of polish Herbert Hoover so pleasantly described, and do the job yourself. The way Charlie and I do is to use a bit of mud, not sand, from the creek bank and rub it on the brass. Then rinse it off and polish the spoon by rubbing it on the side of our hip-boot. An eraser would do as well, but it is more awkward to use and easily lost. The rubber imparts a fine, bright polish to the metal. We tried lacquer but the fishes' teeth were either too sharp or the stones bruised the thin coating, so it never stayed bright for long. Eventually we returned to the bare brass and a few moments of polishing every now and then.

One point in favor of spoons over wooden or plastic under-water lures is: the spoons have a wobbling life-like motion in the water all the time whether being retrieved or just sinking. Did you ever accidentally drop a dime or quarter over board and watch it flutter downward, lost? A lively spoon will do the same. And the flutter will sometimes get a strike when we neglect to begin the retrieve instantly, as we always ought to do.

40

One more thing about the mechanics of the spoon. The split-ring made it possible to turn the tail-hooks up or down depending on the water. If it be full of weeds or snags, it is safer to have the hooks pointing up. But if the water is reasonably clear of treacherous obstacles, let the hooks be pointed downward, for then we will have a hook pointing in each direction at every instant the spoon is in motion, and will hook nearly every fish who tackles it with his mouth open.

Whether or not the first Magic Spoon I showed to Charlie was blessed by Lady Luck I do not know, but it led a long and active life. Its departure was as dramatic as its debut. It caught a muskellunge in the creek where I had never known a muskellunge to swim. In the big lake, one never to be forgotten afternoon, I sat idly watching it swim merrily across a shallow bar, and admiring my handiwork. Out of the corner of an eye I saw something coming like a torpedo, it was another muskellunge. With the rush of an arrow, half in and half out of the water, he crossed the bar, seized the spoon, stopped dead still, then jumped and spit it out. I should have struck, and hard, but I just sat there, benumbed, inert as a sack of oats. Buck fever, and at an age when I should be wearing bi-focals. Revenge was mine, though, within the hour. His brother came from behind, and struck and hooked himself squarely in the tongue with those little trout hooks. He couldn't let go, so we ate him. Then there was the pike who broke my rod when he struck. Snapped it clean at the ferrule. He wasn't much of a fighter. I was wading that afternoon and had a trout net on my shoulder. I got down hip-deep in the creek, let the net drag in the water, played him with the reel and the rod butt, and finally led him up in front of me. He lay still, eyeing me, while I moved the net slowly around in front of his nose, about a foot away. The net began to look awfully small. But I let the line go slack, and with the stub of the rod reached round and tickled him on the tail. It worked. He shot into the net, half of him, anyhow, and I let go the rod and headed for the middle of the cow pasture. We made it, and it was the end of him.

We caught a lot of bass, the Magic Spoon and I. Some big-mouth, mostly small-mouth, but I still carry the scar on my index finger where a small-mouth made a buzz-saw out of my reel handles and laid bare my knuckle-bone before I could get it away. I remember the bass would jump clear over the landing net, out onto the bank, and flopped back into the water while he left the spoon neatly imbedded in a willow root.

But the end came nearly in the same spot as did the beginning, back at the beaver pond. I was alone, casting in the late afternoon, when a lad came along with a .22 hunting frogs, he said. Intent on impressing him with my casting ability, I arched a long, high one, intended for the far shore. It stopped instead in the high branches of a tree. I couldn't shake it loose, so the lad volunteered to shoot the limb down. His aim was good—perfect. He hit the spoon, and it sailed away in to the swamp as the deformed bullet sang a far, mournful, dirge. So ended the colorful career of the first Magic Spoon.

CHAPTER 12

Synthetic Dragon

I HELD THE DRAGON-FLY nymph in my hand and watched its metamorphosis. As I watched the beautiful insect emerge from its water-worn shell and expand in a warm new world, I meditated on it.

It had 'the color of green gold, this insect, but it was infinitely more beautiful, more precious than gold. To hold gold in itself in your hand is thrilling. It can promise food if you are hungry, pleasure if you are fed. But gold is of itself heavy, dead, nothing. The dragon-fly, as it struggled free and walked feebly to the tip of my finger, was alive. It had complete mastery, in its normal life span, of two elements foreign to me: the water and the sky.

When its wings had expanded and dried, it took off in swift sure flight, as confidently as if it had practiced for years. By what miracle did it accomplish this? Where—in under the water—had it learned to fly through the air so swiftly and accurately? I knew it had 'been a proficient swimmer, a voracious predatory creature, in the maze of weeds and muck of the pond water where it had lived and grown. But how could such a creature have spent its time swimming in the water; then emerge and become in a moment master of the air? Its ability to poise in the air, to dart swiftly, and to capture other insects for food, was matched by few birds. And the birds, as fledglings, had all had to learn to fly.

The story of Cinderella was a meager legend compared with the miraculous transformation that had taken place here in the palm of my hand.

I wondered about its brain and how or what it thought. I tried to probe a little way into the mysterious labyrinth we have labeled 'instinct.'

Certainly, it must reason! How else had it known to climb up out of the water when its time came? Was it only instinct that sent it surely after certain other insects for food to sustain it? What made it spend hours searching for a favored spot to deposit its eggs in the water? The dividing line between reasoned and instinctive action has always been nebulous.

But all this was not catching any fish. So, I moved on along the edge of the pond, casting my bass bug. I caught a bass and dressed him out before I creeled him. He had, in his gullet, the remains of a dragonfly nymph; almost the twin of the one I had but recently held. A coincidence, I thought, but something told me it was more than that.

I knew trout ate these nymphs, and I had killed smallmouth bass with them in their bellies. Now I found the bigmouths liked them, too. They were never plentiful, as the may-fly or stone-fly nymphs sometimes were. You never found more than one or two in a fish. Maybe they were harder for the fish to catch. Maybe they were a delicacy any game fish would be eager to eat.

So, the last thought put me off in another inventive mood. The problem was difficult. I could no more make a good counterfeit nymph than I could copy the Cologne Cathedral. Though I had no immediate need for a cathedral; what I wanted was a better artificial fish bait. Had I spent the same amount of time and energy pursuing the coin of the realm, I might have 'become one of Uncle Sam's most valued citizens, around Income Tax time. But when success came, it had to remain its own reward, and Uncle Sam the loser.

For a long time, I sought to imitate the nymph exactly. Eventually it occurred to me I was foolish to try to copy such a complex insect with fur and silk and feathers. I could not make one good enough to fool a man, let alone a fish. And were not a fish eyes much better adapted to inspecting such things?

Finally, I met the magician. He could prove things are not always as they seem. The way he tricked people gave me an idea. If he could make half-a-dozen pigeons fly out of a hat that looked hardly big enough to contain one small canary, or saw a beautiful girl in half; it was only a matter of illusion. He performed no miracles. His was all trickery.

He gave me the word "illusion." In fishing was not the polished metal spoon or spinner merely an illusion? And though the spoons and spinners did not even remotely resemble minnows, they fooled a lot of fish. So why not devise a lure to give the illusion of the dragon-fly nymph without necessarily copying it?

I had caught two nymphs, put them in a gold-fish bowl, and fed them raw meat. Maybe I did not feed them enough, for one day the one ate the other, and left me one to study. And in a little while he crawled out of the bowl, spread his wings and flew away. But he left one clue that had previously escaped me. All these nymphs had a horny shell something like a crawfish. It seemed to me, if I could find a flashy substitute for this horny shell material, I might have an answer to my problem.

Then I had an answer. Santa Claus brought me a package wrapped in brown cellophane. The color and texture of the translucent material almost exactly matched the clean, discarded shell of the nymph. To this day I cannot recall which necktie was in that package.

At any rate, I set about devising a fly wrapped in colored cellophane. And before long I had a bait that really fooled the fish. It looked no more like a nymph than a hundred others I had tied, but it caught smart fish, where the others had failed.

It is a fly, wrapped and tied in the time-honored fashion; not a cork bug or molded lure. The most fastidious fly fisherman can use it without his conscience troubling him. A dry-fly "purist" can use it, for it will float better than the average dry-fly if correctly tied. Its built-in buoyancy is most necessary to its success as a wet-fly, for it adds to its lively swimming action in deep water.

From the several seasons we have fished this fly and the dozens of variations of it we have tried, our most successful color and shape is the one I shall describe. Though variations in color, in distant waters, might add to its effectiveness.

Whether you tie your own flies, buy them ready made, or have them tied to your order, the few moments it will take to read the nymph's description may be worthwhile, for we feel some day this bug or an improvement of it will rank with the Royal Coachman in popularity. By our own experience, it has taken educated trout which had previously turned away from the Royal Coachman.

Let's pause a moment with the Royal Coachman, long the most popular fly pattern among fishermen. It resembles no particular insect. Its popularity stems entirely from its good looks. And while it has hooked thousands of fish over the years, it has also caught the fancy of a multitude of fishermen. We might well consider this point. Any trout fly pattern must first catch a fisherman before it can possibly hook a fish. How would a fly ever become attached to the tip of the fisherman's leader if it did not catch his fancy first? So, the fisherman must first be caught, and then the fish, regardless of the fly pattern.

Enough of that. If you want to tie one of these nymphs for yourself, assemble a list of material as follows:

No. 8 dry-fly hook
white woolen yarn
tan or brown tying thread
wood duck or dyed mallard feathers
brown hackle
gold wire or narrow gold tinsel
celluloid cement
brown colored cellophane

Now by referring to the sketch, Fig. 1, set the hook in the vise and attach the gold wire or tinsel as indicated. Tie on the wool and wind loosely to form the shape of the body as in Fig. 2. This must be somewhat larger than the finished body for our cellophane wrapping will compress it. Now fold the end of a one-eighth inch strip of the cellophane and tie it in at the front of the body. Spiral it back and then forward, molding the wool into the plump finished shape as in Fig. 3 and Fig. 4. Bring the gold wire or tinsel forward tightly, binding the body as in Fig. 5. Endeavor to have the body completely covered with two thickness of the cellophane and ridged by the wire as in Fig. 5. Six turns of the wire work out best. The live insects have nine prominent segments, but nine turns of wire added extra weight and tended to cut the cellophane by creasing it too sharply. I give some trout credit for a good bit of man taught intelligence, but, even after nearly forty years fishing, I cannot bring myself to believe any of them can work problems in arithmetic. Six turns of the tinsel or wire will round up a nice body, slightly compressible to the fingers, and with enough air trapped in the yarn to keep it buoyant.

Now set the fly, as half completed, up out of the way and coat it with the cement. While it dries start another for you are going to need more than one, unless you fish with a very heavy leader or in a stream where there are none but baby trout!

FIG. 1.

FIG. 2.

FIG. 3.

FIG. 4.

FIG. 5.

FIG. 6.

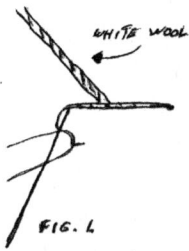

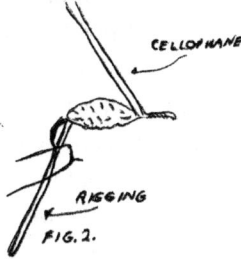

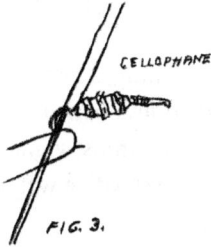

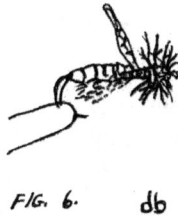

When the cement is set, tie in the wood duck feather and the hackle, like Fig. 5. Divide the wood duck fibers and by crisscrossing the tying thread make them lay along each side of the body, not atop it like wings. These fibers are not to represent wings but to give the impression that his breathing and swimming apparatus are working in good order. Now hold the feather back and bind it down as in Fig. 6. Finish off his thorax with the wool, cellophane, and gold wire, spiral three or four turns of hackle over it, then bring the wood duck feather forward overall and finish off the head. Cement the head, admire your work, and try to think of a good excuse for going fishing.

Because we used a light-weight hook and trapped a lot of air in the now water-tight body, the fly will float like a cork bass bug. And cast a lot easier. Beyond that, it will sometimes catch bass when bigger lures fail. It needs no oiling to keep it on the surface. Of course, after some fish have chewed on it for a while, it may spring a leak and sink. That is another reason why I suggested you make more than one at a time.

We fish the nymph as we would any dry-fly. Just letting it drift along with the current, and drifting it several times over each likely looking spot, or casting to the rise if there is no definite hatch of insects on the water. Let it tumble along in swift water then twitch it slowly out of the quiet eddies. When there is no sign of activity on the surface, and we feel the fish are lying deep, we fish deep by adding a bit of lead to the leader a foot or so above the fly. Let him swim slowly down then work back toward the surface. Watch like a hawk, and be ready and eager to strike at any unnatural movement of the line or leader.

Because our nymph is slightly soft and yielding, a fish will retain it on his tongue longer than he would a hard-bodied fly. So, he is easier to hook on the surface. But deep fishing will require the utmost vigilance if it is to pay dividends. To probe the bottom of a deep pool with a wet or sunken fly is a difficult method of fishing, but it catches big fish.

In my younger, more agile days, I used to catch grass-hoppers and fish them deep with a small hook and a bit of lead. Our trout streams usually became low and warm and crystal clear in the grass-hopper months, and the trout would congregate in the deep spring-fed pools.

Hopper fishing had its disadvantages. You had to catch the hoppers, and, on the very days the trout were biting best, the hoppers were most active, and devilishly quick in eluding you. You lost a lot of hoppers casting. You had to let the fish gorge the bait before you struck, not knowing whether he was big or little, and so you killed a good many small trout with your grasshoppers you could have released unhurt had you hooked them on an artificial fly. I have yet to encounter a fish ignorant enough to swallow an artificial bait, so the percentage of fatalities among the small fry has greatly decreased since I forsook chasing grass-hoppers.

When my imitation insect tricks a fish so he closes his mouth upon it, and sometimes snags himself in the tongue, I am satisfied. From there it is but a matter of persuading him into the landing net either to be killed or returned to grow some more.

Breath-taking experiences with the synthetic nymph have been many and varied. Probably nothing in the whole category of angling can make a man's heart out more dido's than the sudden appearance of a big trout under his fly. For years we hunted big trout with large bucktail or streamer flies, casting repeatedly over likely spots, occasionally rewarded with the flash of a big one as he inspected, but rarely struck the lure. Then spent hours and days trying to catch that particular fish. Sometimes we did, more often we did not, but the nymph has changed all this since it assumed the role of big fish finder. With it, the flash often means a strike, and a battle.

If I sound overly enthusiastic about my own artificial bug, it is only because it had been successful beyond my expectations. Certainly, a fly pattern that will trick overgrown specimens of the trout and bass family deserves a wide use. Big fish ought to be caught and little ones left to grow, if fishing in civilized places is to remain interesting.

In closing, let us return for a moment to the original inspiration for all this, the dragon-fly nymph and his amazing metamorphosis. It, like man, inhabits nearly every part of the earth, excepting only the polar regions. In this he possibly shows more sense than man. According to the fossil hunters, he was here, like the fishes, long before man put in his appearance. Whatever he may think of man, the fisherman, is a point best left uninvestigated. Man's inflated ego still remains his most necessary possession.

In the matter of names, dragon-fly now seems to be the commonly accepted English version. But it was not always so. When I was a curious, questioning boy, my elders called him the Devil's Darning Needle' or 'Snake Feeder'. Some British folk call him 'Horse-Stinger'. The Frenchmen have given him a pretty name 'Demoiselle'. And a few miles north and east the Hollanders have a name for the dragon-fly, "Scherpstekendevlieg!" It only goes to prove that even in the small matter of naming an insect, there is a lot of truth in the old saying, "You can't beat the Dutch".

CHAPTER 13

Fly Fishing

PROBABLY MANY OF YOU will not remember very much about the horse-and buggy days. But whenever I try to explain the rudiments of fishing with flies, the first picture to cross my mind is that of old John, who pumped the oil wells. Many a June evening I climbed into his buggy, relaxed on the oily cushion, and watched his patient mare toil up the long hill toward home. John loved the woods, where he worked alone, but he had no time to fish, he said. Now time is nothing to him, and I hope and trust he has trout water and tackle to enjoy it. If I knew his kindly nature, he will fish with barbless hooks and put the trout back gently, and unhurt.

As we rode along in the evening, his whip was a part of him. It moved continually. illustrating his conversation, and all the time deftly flicking flies from the mare's rump. The little tassel on the tip of his whip danced as we rode, now touching the horse, now flying in the air. Like a trout fly over a riffle, it caressed the mare's flanks, dipping and rising, effortlessly. So gentle were its movements as it flicked away the irritating flies, I knew the mare had never felt the sting of a whip in anger by old John's hand.

The buggy whip was a thin, lithe thing. If it fitted the driver's hand, it was an accurate, responsive extension of his arm. It could chase the flies daintily or it could strike like a viper, with lightning speed and stinging strength.

Now let us define a good fly-fishing rod. It should be a thin, powerful weapon. If it fits its owner's hand it will cast a fly daintily, then if need be, strike like a snake, with lightning speed. A fly rod must be a delicate tool if it is to cast an artificial fly to the trout with any of the airy, weightless grace of the live insect it imitates.

If it feels in any way top-heavy or if it requires a conscious effort to cast with it, don't buy it. It will only tire your arm along the stream. Fly fishing should be the hobby a man pursues to rebuild his strength, not wear it down. There are long and heavy fly rods which will cast a heavy line well beyond a hundred feet, but the energy burned to accomplish this distance comes from the muscles of the fisherman, not from the rod. It is a good deal like work to fish with such equipment.

So, the fly rod I would have you use will feel like a fairy wand in your hand. A fellow can fish all day, if he likes, without tiring wrist, arm or shoulder. It will cast lightly and accurately thirty, forty or at the most, fifty feet. And that is plenty far enough for trout flies. If the fish is farther away than fifty feet it is up to the fisherman to move closer rather than attempt an accurate cast that may fail, and only frighten him.

I do not believe you can err on the side of delicacy in purchasing a fly rod for trout fishing. The smallest and lightest one I ever saw weighed a bare two ounces, was six and a half feet long, and cast an 'H' line twenty-five or thirty feet. More of a toy than a fishing rod, it had surprising strength, and its owner caught a lot of fish on it. But he was an expert. Fly rods for us ordinary fishermen, I would say, should weigh between three and one-half and five ounces and be from seven and one-half to nine feet long. The length and weight to be chosen, of course, by whoever intends to do the fishing. And the bigger man will naturally choose a longer heavier rod.

But, can I cast bass bugs or spinner fly combinations with light fly rods like these, you ask? And I reply, bugs and spinners are not trout flies, they require stronger rods. Fly fishing is the lighter, easier way of fishing. So, choose a light rod for fly fishing and make light work of it.

First the rod. Now the line. Fully as important to the effortless ease of fly casting as the rod. Like the flexible end on the tip of old John's whip, the line is the vital link between 'the man and the fly. Plug casting, we learned to toss the plug and let the line follow it. Fly casting, we have no weight to toss so we think back to John's flicking buggy whip. Our fly rod, line, leader and fly add up to nothing more than an elongated version of his 'whip. We can vary the reach of it by lengthening or shortening the line. So, the line is the vital link in the whole assembly, for it is the only part that is variable. Whether we cast ten feet or a hundred, the rod, leader and fly remain the same; only the line varies in length and weight. That is why it is so very important to have a line of just the proper size and weight.

Where the line is too thin or light it will not straighten out smoothly when cast. A breeze will throw it off its course. Applying more power will make it zip around, but spoils accuracy and the fisherman's temper. A too heavy line will straighten out quickly and be determined to fall toward the water or tangle in the bushes. It means a continual fight to keep it high in the air, clear of obstacles. The line that fits the rod, or rather becomes a smooth working part of the casting assembly, will do as we wish, smoothly and with no great exertion on our part.

To purchase such a line as this, it is best to be guided by the rod maker's catalogue or the salesman from whom the rod was bought. However, they are not infallible, so I suggest if the line they advise does not suit, try one a size or two smaller. The reason this works so often, is simple. The recommendations are written up by expert casters, who know how to cast unbelievably long distances. To achieve distance, the heavier line helps, but to us who are striving for delicacy and accuracy at short range, a thinner line works better.

The rod, the line, and now the reel. In the beginning, fly fishermen got along without it. It was invented later. A step on the rutted road of human progress, the reel. Some are automatic, some are stem-wind, though they all serve but one purpose, to hold the line we are not using at the moment.

Since the reel was invented, whole books have been written about its usefulness as a counter-balance on the butt of a fly rod. Arguments have waxed warm over the pendulum action of a fly nod in casting, with various weights of reels attached. But, no matter, a bit of common sense has solved more weighty problems.

The analogy of the whip can be carried over into this problem of the proper fly reel. John's whip had no counter-balance beyond his hand. It had a leaden weight in the grip which heightened the illusion of delicacy and responsiveness in the tip. The weight was directly under his fingers, not beyond his hand in either direction. A fly rod has the same stiffness under the hand, but extra weight is never added, as in the whip, for the reel is expected to provide the weight. The difficulty, and the source of all the argument, is because the weight is added, not under the hand, but behind it so it acts as a counter-balance.

D'Artagnan, show these confused fly fishermen a rapier. Show them how its handle is solid and weighty, its point thin, sharp and alive to your wishes. John, let them try your buggy whip, show them how it can be so gentle and caressing or strike with stinging power.

Because the sword and the whip were more necessary to the forward (?) march of the human race, their invention antedated that of our fly reels and our 'fysshing' rods. And since the rod was made before the reel, the reel's inventor had no alternative but to stick it on behind. But the heavier it is, the more it will spoil the responsiveness of your fly rod. Many manufacturing fishermen concur with me in this. Witness their designs of new and lighter weight reels.

One friend of mine became so convinced my arguments were correct, he made a belt around his waist and fastened his reel to it. So far as I could judge, he cast and handled his line as well with the reel on the belt as on the rod. But one day I saw him hook a trout. Cranking away at the reel against his tummy, and holding his rod high with his other hand, he looked for all the world like an organ grinder with a monkey on a leash. Had he a tin cup and a larger audience, he might have made some money!

So, the rod casts easier and smoother without a reel, or with one weighing as little as possible. With any kind of compromise, such as this, allowances have to be considered, so if the convenience of an automatic reel or the possible need for greater line length to cope with the runs of heavy fish out-weigh the advantages of a little light-weight spool, each angler must study his own problem, and decide accordingly.

My own fly-fishing equipment, simmered through many more seasons than I like to count, has boiled down to these items: three and one-half ounce rod, size 'F' or 'G' line and a very light and fragile aluminum reel. The rod is seven and one-half feet long and of what is described as 'wet-fly' action—softer, slower and more resilient than the quick, stiff 'dry-fly' rods now so commonly offered for sale. I buy level casting lines for the more expensive taper gives no advantage at the short ranges I cast, twenty to forty or fifty feet. Because I never need more than sixty feet of casting line to extend my equipment to its utmost, I cut it off at twenty yards and fill the spool of my reel with as much fine bait-casting line as it will hold, underneath the polished fly line. With it, I have a total line length of fifty or sixty yards, enough to meet most any emergency.

For the light running line, or backing, I have lately come to use only those woven from synthetic fibers for they do not mildew or rot as did the pure silk. Nine- or ten-pound test is more than adequate, remembering that fine leader tippets and the knots tied therein hardly ever will withstand a dead weight pull of more than three or four pounds.

My greatest difficulty has always been to find reels light as a feather yet strong, dependable and closely fitted so my line could not become pinched or tangled between spool and frame.

All in all, by the process of trial and rejection, my fly-fishing tackle became, down through the years, continually lighter and more delicate, until it reached the ineducable minimum of strength and casting ability. To go any lighter would sacrifice ability to fight the fish or to offer flies to them on the larger wadable streams. As to the fighting ability of my light rod, I can easily apply, with it, all the pressure a trout leader dare withstand. With a six-ounce rod or a telegraph pole, I could do no more. So, I wade along, fishing with a little rod and reel weighing hardly more than six ounces altogether, fishing easily, casting flies that drop lightly and life-like onto the water. This way, it is fun to fly-fish, but if the tackle is too heavy, it can only be work.

So much for the fly-fishing tackle. Leaders and flies must be considered later, separately. If any fisherman of experience has traveled the same course of fly casting down the years, and come up with different conclusions as to the practicality of light weight rod and reel for trout, he is certainly entitled to a hearing. I am but trying to give you an idea of the pleasure to be had along the trout streams, using easily handled equipment. With a long and heavy rod, it will be difficult to cast lightly and daintily. It will be difficult to negotiate the tangled thickets where the finest trout always hide. And finally, none of us fish long and steadily enough nowadays to develop the muscles we use in casting. That is, to a degree that will let us handle a long and heavy rod without tiring unduly.

I do not mean for anyone to become obsessed with the idea that the lightest possible tackle is the only kind to use. Far from it. I mean only for those who may have tried fly fishing with wrong tackle and have become discouraged, to try again with the tools I have outlined.

Fly fishing is unquestionably the most perfect outdoor sport man has ever invented. Walking, wading and casting will loosen and relax every muscle in a man's body in a few hours. It will try his intelligence, his patience and his temper, and freshen them all. It is perhaps the only sport a man can indulge to the limits of his spare time and strength without its palling or slackening in interest or harming him, physically.

As with the bait-casting, this is not intended to give step by step directions on the how of fly casting. You learn best by watching others and by fishing. We only mean to point out a few of the pit-falls along the way. The first thing to consider, then, is the fly, the artificial fly. It should alight on the water as lightly as the natural insect. So, in aiming a cast, a fisherman never casts directly at the water but always at an imaginary spot a foot or two above it. The fly stops its forward motion and falls onto the water, not slapping the surface. Sounds simple, and once learned, is automatic with the angler, but it is one of the hardest points a beginner has to master. It is one of the little things having to do with catching fish.

Too, like the plug caster, the fly fisherman must have eyes in the back of his head. And good sharp ones, or he will find there is more hot water to get into along an icy trout stream than he ever realized. His hack swing covers much more territory than the bait-caster's; territory always seeming to be crowded with trees and bushes. With practice, and with nothing but practice, the persistent angler will someday discover that the eyes in the back of his head provide him with a continual moving picture of the terrain and the shrubbery that lies behind him. The briars and tree limbs behind him will, for a long time, be the makings of many a first-rate nightmare. But with experience, at first vaguely and often in error, the picture will come. And with each succeeding season become clearer and more accurate until at last, unexpectedly, he will realize that he truly has good eyes in the back of his head, in defiance of all the optical rules.

Many times, the embryo angler finds himself in a spot where he is ringed around with nature's tangled flora, a patch of open water before him, and a good trout surely lurking if he could only cast his fly a bit further. So, remembering the old buggy whip, with which John could not make a back cast when the buggy top was up, he whips the rod sharply forward and down. Lo and behold, the line, a little longer than the rod, describes a cart-wheel and rolls straight out to its mark on the water. Experienced fishermen use the Roll Cast probably more than any other, for they know the good trout are most likely to be hiding in the spots too tough for amateurs to cast into, on hard fished streams.

One point about the Roll Cast most copybooks neglect to mention; the rod does not necessarily have to be in a vertical or upright position to start the cast. Often an over-hanging branch prevents a vertical rod position. Good casts can be made with a rod angle down to 45 degrees provided the line is retrieved a bit faster and the rod whipped at a crossing downward angle. A good billiard player would probably get the knack of angling his Roll Cast quicker than anyone else, since it requires one angle to offset another in order to reach the target under these conditions.

Just as the golfer has his hooks and slices, his good and bad days, so can the fly fisherman seek the key to perfection in his fly casting, but with no more chance of ever finding it. One advantage he has over the golfer, though, is hooks and slices are acceptable parts of his casting repertoire, and when he tosses a lucky curve, he can persuade himself that he meant to do it just that way.

Curve casts catch a lot of fish. Righthand curves, left-hand curves and slack line casts are all useful additions to his bag of tricks. The dry-fly addicts practice them assiduously. But do not be mis-led, they all help in wet-fly fishing, too. With dry-flies, it is easy to see how the fly drifts more naturally where a proper curve of the line is laid out on the water. Wet-flies should drift along, too. Because they imitate either drowned insects or nymphs, or caddis flies descending, they should drift along, buffeted by the action of the current against fly and leader. A tiny twitch now and then where the current is lazy is permissible, but the swift jerking you may see some fellows practicing is rarely needed. To prove this point? Some evening when the Mayflies are rising and the trout jumping round about you, exercise all your will-power, quit fishing, wade out into the water and watch the insects swimming to the surface, tumbled by the current. A few moments watching the live insects will plant one thought firmly in the mind, an artificial fly should tumble and roll and drift with the current.

Now we come to the final end point of all fly fishing; establishing the connection between fly and fish, or hooking the trout who rose to the fly. It has engendered endless discussions, this business of striking the rise and hooking the fish. New beginners are usually baffled by the swiftness of small trout in sampling and rejecting artificial flies. Sometimes they came away with a conviction that it just is not humanly possible to catch such trout with artificial flies and fly rods.

But it is not as difficult as that. If it were, our civilized fishing waters would contain many more fish than they actually do nowadays. In a great majority of cases the trout hooks himself with no help from the fly fisherman. Any tautness of line and leader, as in casting down and across a current or retrieving a fly through still water, is sufficient to imbed the barb of a small fly where the fish has closed his mouth upon it. Under these conditions, if fish rise to the fly repeatedly but are not hooked, it only means that the fly has some attraction for them but is not good enough an imitation to fool them completely. The remedy is obvious, try another fly, or a smaller one of the same pattern.

A floating fly with a slack line requires action from the angler to set the barb. Action without conscious effort. It is like pulling the trigger of a shotgun, shooting at a fast flying bird. You do it, but you cannot remember telling your finger when or how to do it. Exact timing is, however, not nearly so important in flying fishing as in shot-gunning. You can be a tenth of a second late in your strike and easily hook your fish, if he really wanted the fly. So, curb your eagerness, take him calmly, and very soon you will have the knack. Nine-tenths of the problem of hooking trout with artificial flies is solved when the exactly correct fly is on the tip of your leader.

By this time, it is evidently plain the light fly rod is my favorite fishing rod. Given time and fresh water containing fish, I can find some sport. Most any kind of fish will serve, they need not be trout. For instance, in clear water a school of feeding suckers and a few small wet flies drifted down among them can start a lot of excitement. It's a difficult game. They have an excellent sense of smell or taste and can inhale a little fly, and blow it out again almost faster than your eye can follow. And carp will do the same. If a man is Indian enough to steal close to a school of rooting carp, he may hook one on a wet fly. Ever since I tangled with a fifteen pounder one hot day, I have carefully avoided them. Tackle busters!

Bullheads, when they school up near the surface of a shallow pond, are easy prey for trout flies, and perch, sunnies and rock bass are ready to play most any old time. Big-mouthed bass, sometimes eager and sometimes maddeningly deliberate, are fair game. And on lazy August afternoons I have killed small-mouths by careful stalking and a drifting wet trout fly when nothing else would do the trick. I have been known to go out fly fishing and come home with a half-dozen bull-frogs, caught on trout tackle.

But the fairest game of all along the water are water snakes. When you see one swimming, cast a foot or so beyond him and strike. If you miss, you will likely have another chance. And if you snag him near the head or the tail, it will not be much trouble to land him and convert him into a good snake, by bashing his brains out. But hook a big one right in the middle and you may have trouble. All in all, water snakes are very fair game for the fly fisherman. One dead snake means many live fish. So, every exciting victory a fisherman can claim over the water snake tribe, will someday provide the wherewithal to declare a dividend in fish, to repay him.

Just as the rabbit hunter occasionally shoots an owl, and gloats over it, the fisherman will derive a great deal more pleasure in destroying the snake than he would in killing one more trout. The hunter with his owl usually rushes to the nearest taxidermist, has his trophy stuffed, and displays it proudly on the mantel-piece. Rightly so. The wise fisherman will destroy the water snake when he can, and his fly-rod is a good weapon for the purpose, but he will bury it and go on about his business. To ask the taxidermist to stuff it or attempt to persuade a housewife to let him display a water snake on her dining room wall, might endanger his whole fishing future. Best catch the snake, kill it, and say nothing.

The most picturesque pool along my creek is the swimming hole. The creek angles into a sharp fold in the hill. It has swept a clean, deep pool, with a fine sandy beach on the low side. The steep hill, acting in self-preservation, has dropped a ring of huge sand-stone boulders at its base. On a summer Sunday afternoon, the pool is filled with shrieking, splashing children. Anxious mammas hover along the edge, and bored papas, who find no peace and rest in the arms of Mother Nature here, saunter nervously about the picnic grove.

Big trout live in the swimming hole. Maybe because it is the deepest pool along the creek, or because of the cold springs running in from the base of the hill. Possibly, they relish the activity of the humans on Sunday afternoons. The tumbled boulders provide safe caverns beneath the water where the fish can hide and watch the kids cavort.

I stood hip-deep in the pool at sunrise of a June morning, watching for a trout to rise. Instead I caught a rustling in the leaves at the base of the hill and saw a black snake slither down into the water and begin to swim across. When it was about forty feet away, and broadside, I cast across it, let my fly sink a moment, and struck. As the hook bit in, it thrashed and turned. Maybe it thought I was an island in the midst of all the water. It came at me and as the military say, I withdrew to consolidate my position. Frankly, I retreated in haste and in bad order. The snake was gaining rapidly as I hit the sandy beach and started looking for a club. Somehow, the closer the snake came toward me the bigger it looked, and my three and one-half ounce rod seemed entirely inadequate as a weapon of defense. On the sand, I could run as fast as it could, and I did. But I gained a momentary advantage when the fly, imbedded in its side, caught in the weeds. With a charred ember from the picnic fireplace, I delivered a blow I will never forget, nor it remember. After a while I measured it. It was five feet and ten inches long.

And definitely the longest cold-blooded creature I had ever hooked with my little fly rod.

Some folks will condemn me for killing a black snake, I know. Some already have, but before you do, come along trout fishing with me in the spring, when everything is fresh and new and clean. When the birds are singing about their eggs and fledglings, and the squirrels are busy with their babies. The fly fisherman moves leisurely, quietly along his trout stream. He hears the voices of the birds, bragging and scolding. He learns to recognize the friendly annoyance in a squirrel's chattering down at him. The bright flash of a bird's wing, the squirrel's plume jerking in unison to his chatter, are but a part of the perfect sport of angling. Then, someday he will hear the birds or the squirrels crying in distress, and because he has come to love their presence along the stream, he will recognize the call and investigate. He may discover, as we have, a black snake eating the eggs of a ruffed grouse, or a pair of squirrels racing frantically up and down as a black snake climbs high in the tree approaching the cavity where the helpless babies lie. And I have no doubt you will do as we have done, kill the snake. I would rather see a mother grouse with her chicks, working through the woods, talking to them with her little chirps, they sound like polished grains of wheat strung on a shiny silver wire, than all the black snakes in the country.

So, when we sum it all up, fly-fishing is the perfect outdoor sport. It has stood the test of time, since our immortal Izaak's day. And how fortunate we are to live in this scientific age, which gave us our rubber boots and water-proof waders, the aluminum for feather-weight reels, and our dainty yet so powerful fly-fishing rods.

Is it any wonder that Izaak, with his heavy rod and wet feet, gave up fly-fishing once in a while, and sat under a tree with a dough-ball on his hook?

CHAPTER 14

Susquehanna "Salmon"

ALIAS: PICKEREL, PIKE, PERCH, Yellow Pike, Walleye Pike

The Allegheny is a beautiful river. Placid, dainty, and sparkling under a summer sun, she seems innocent as a trout brook. Filled with crashing, roaring ice in a spring breakup, she is a terrible monster capable of awful destruction. In late fall, swollen, black, and sullen, absorbing the millions of silent snowflakes that blot out the farther shore, she is as mysterious as the sea. And more ominous, for she is so utterly silent then.

But the Allegheny is the habitat of walleyes, or if you please, Susquehanna salmon, and upon that pertinent fact hangs this tale.

How old I was when I saw my first walleye I do not remember. Age, in years, was of little importance to a small boy. I must have been pretty young, perhaps knee-high to a wash-tub, for it is a washtub full of fish that I remember.

In those days Allegheny fishermen were practical men. They hauled a flat-boat several miles upstream, rigged a wire basket on iron rods over one end of the boat, and, armed with long barbed spears, the basket flaming with tow saturated in kerosene, descended the river in the night, spearing 'salmon' as they came.

Such procedure is, naturally, highly illegal now and with good reason, for we have too many fishermen. To share equally our pleasure, we must restrain ourselves. But let it be said in defense of this old and exciting way of fishing that no small fry were killed or injured. Only mature fish were taken, though some of these were doubtless badlywounded and escaped.

A little older, and with clearer memory, I remember my first ice gorge along the Allegheny. The up-river ice broke and started down and down-river ice held firm. The best example extant of what actually happens when irresistible force meets immovable object, the ice jammed tightly, crashing, climbing, and smashing back upon itself, flooding the lowlands as the river became choked with packing ice.

It was a particularly savage ice gorge, for the river lacked sufficient flow to float the ice away. Finally, however, in the long black hour before dawn, the water cut through and the flood subsided. But the ice remained, piled high above the normal water level and pushed up onto the lowlands along both sides of the river. And it was in the crevasses of this ice-pack, a few days later, that we first discovered the fish. Walleyes were packed in among the tumbled cakes of river ice, stiff with frost themselves, and huge carp and suckers, too.

We boys and the corner grocer fared exceedingly well in the next few days. A two-pound walleye could be exchanged for a nickel, (sometimes a little haggling brought a dime) from almost any fish hungry housewife. The grocer got the nickels, we got, possibly, more candy than was good for us. It was an exciting time, and we boys made the most of it. In later years I have often wondered how it happened that we escaped injury as we explored the tumbled masses of river ice.

After several days, however, the supply of fish became exhausted and we were forced back upon more hum-drum methods of obtaining candy money—snow-shoveling, ash-emptying, etc.

The ice melted slowly. Without any exact memory of dates, I remember that the violets were blooming and sucker fishermen were lazying on the river bank in the warm spring sunshine before the last ice was gone. As the ice disappeared more and more dead fish became exposed on the flat land along the river. A distinct memory of the odor of those decaying fish is still with me, as well as the fact that of all the kinds of fish in the river, only three species were trapped in the ice, the 'salmon' and suckers and carp.

The Allegheny was the home of thousands of small mouth bass at that time. And though there are perhaps more bass in the river now than a half century ago, there were plenty then. But none were trapped in the ice gorge. And that should bear out our contention that in the Allegheny, at least, small mouths hide under rocks in the deepest water in the winter.

It is a long jump from spring and melting river ice, violets and spring sunshine, to fall and November snow-flurries, to 'salmon' fishing with its freezing tackle and drift wood fires; but we can jump it easily via the lino-type machine. I do not believe there were as many fishermen per thousand population at the turn of the century as there are today. But it seems, looking back, that if those early fishermen were few in numbers, they were all the more persistent in practicing the art.

Every day in the fall, after school let out, we boys raced to the river to inspect the day's catch. And we could count on the same small group of fishermen, around the same small fire, day after day all through November. What those men did to earn a living I'll never know. If they had a formula that permitted them to fish all the time, without ever working, it died with them, and what a pity!

They all used similar tackle, and for late fall fishing with minnows their tackle has never been improved upon. The rod was a natural cane, twelve or fourteen feet long. Some had been cut and ferrules fitted. Most were in one solid length. Some were heat-treated in fancy mottled patterns. (You can do this for yourself by patient and careful manipulation over a gas flame.) Many rods used little screw-eyes for line guides, though some guides were of bent wire, taped on.

About that time, I was sporting a brass single action reel; and the polished nickel, quadruple-multiplying, hundred-yard capacity reels of the 'salmon' fishermen fascinated me. They whirred so smoothly I itched to own one. But when I finally got one, I neglected it, the sand got inside it, and it was soon useless.

I think the lines were mostly of twisted linen, though I cannot be sure. Hard braided silk should work as well as the linen; but for this kind of fishing modern nylon is taboo. River fishing, big-river fishing (the Allegheny is 200 yards wide in our town) calls for plenty of line, at least 100 yards. When a 'salmon' takes the bait, he may not run so far, but, if there is a current in the water, you must let the fish take line so long as he wants to move. And thus, the more current, the bigger belly in the line when you lift the rod to strike. Elastic nylon works well enough (in the heavier sizes) where you have a straight taunt line, but where you have a long curve in the line, this elasticity makes it difficult to set a hook.

It is this long curve in the line that, necessitates the twelve- or four-teen-foot rod. When you strike, you have to take up a lot of slack, and a short plug-casting rod cannot give you the leverage to do it.

The long cane rod has other advantages for river bait-fishing. It permits a long, sweeping two-handed cast, a la surf fishing; a cast that starts the minnow slowly and lands him gently far out in the river. It permits fastening the sinker two or three feet up the line from the hook so the bait has a chance to move about the river bottom when he descends to walleye headquarters.

Too, in freezing weather the long rod, held high, helps keep the water away from the guides and the reel where it has such a nasty habit of freezing and gumming the works. And if or when the line becomes frozen fast in the guides, dipping the rod in the water will quickly melt the ice and release it. That does not apply to the reel, however. When it becomes frozen, you thaw it by the fire or go home.

Dipping a fishing rod under water to thaw out the line and free the guides is an old trick, of course. It is all very well to try it with a long and inexpensive cane pole. I do not advise it for your expensive split bamboo.

Since this is a little yarn of recollections, I think a memory of one bitter morning, opening day of trout season, would not be amiss. Charlie and I met the big city angler along the brook. He was discouraged. There was a ball of ice like a golf ball at a tip of his beautiful fly-rod and a just as big ball of ice round a bunched-up worm on his hook.

Kind-hearted Charlie told him to hold the rod-tip and the hook under water and the ice would melt away. A look of absolute disbelief spread over the amateur's face.

As I went on down-stream, Charlie launched into a long-winded, highly technical, and finally somewhat impatient discussion of the phenomenon. The last words heard were:

"Damit, man, running water don't freeze! If it froze, it couldn't run."

Come to think of it, opening day is not so very far away.

CHAPTER 15

Spring Fever

THE FOLLOWING PARAGRAPH WAS printed in a box next to this article in the March 1947 issue of the Pennsylvania Angler Magazine.

> VITAL STATISTICS: Don Blair was 41 years old on Aug. 1, 1946. Born in Franklin, Pa., he has lived in and near it all his life. Graduated from high school—never learned to spell or to punctuate a sentence. Worked as a clerk for the N. Y. C. R. R. two years; then as an auto mechanic, and finally in 1925 began career as a radio repairman. Worked twenty years and quit. Owns home, small income, two dogs, and some chickens. Can't count chickens, nor keep his checkbook in agreement with the bank's figures. Family composed of wife, Helen, and daughter, Judy, age seven. Both have red hair.

When I was a youngster, grandmother's favorite remedy for spring fever was a potion of sulfur and molasses. When I grew a little older, I discovered a more pleasant, and most likely more effective remedy in sucker fishing.

Each year the fever commenced with the first breath of warm south wind and grew until opportunity presented itself to go fishing. Fishing was the antidote. But it could not be called a remedy; for while it soothed the fever, it failed to effect any permanent cure.

Any definition of sucker fishing must, of course, begin by noting that it is an outdoor sport. But the word, sport, suggests vigor and action. Sucker fishing brings a picture of quiet enjoyment, rarely vigorous, and supposing a minimum of action. The first warm south wind, a fragrant driftwood fire, shrinking snow-banks, and, possibly least important of all, a gentle nibbling and tugging at the baited hook, these are sucker fishing.

And if anticipation is the mainspring of human activity; where on earth is a better place to indulge it than the bank of a quiet brook, with the first faint whispering of spring stirring the grass roots?

The suckers in my bailiwick do a lot of traveling, spring and fall. They migrate. They winter in deep, quiet eddies in the Allegheny (River). They gather round the mouths of its tributary creeks and brooks with the first hint of spring. Then upstream they go whenever warm rain swells the smaller streams.

Suckers can and will travel a long way on these spring migrations. In one shallow stream, the fish move up fifteen miles in a very short time. Just how fast they travel is a point a life-time of study has not permitted me to clarify. Muddy waters always prevent accurate noting of their starting time. Somehow, though, I am nearly convinced that the journey is sometimes completed in a single night.

The suckers' purpose in traveling, of course, is to spawn; to deposit the eggs on suitable shallow riffles. That duty accomplished, there remains for the fish a pleasant summer spent browsing. In this connection, let it be noted that the suckers hold a similar position in the stream economy to the rabbits or the deer of the forest. All are prolific creatures. Some grow to maturity; but in nature's scheme of things, the great majority of the small fry are consumed as food by superior predators. Their principal reason for being is to convert the grass, the green stuff, into flesh.

And so, the suckers rank primarily as food fishes. They are not so important or so highly prized by the angling fraternity as are the predatory fishes. But as a remedy for spring fever the suckers hold a rightfully important place in the fisherman's calendar. If they accomplished nothing more than to get the angler outdoors in the early spring; to spur him into spading a part of his garden, hunting worms, that would be enough. But suckers provide delicious food besides their recreational importance.

Like any other wild creatures, these fish require some knowledge and cunning on the part of the angler if pursuit is to end in capture. Tackle is not so important as knowledge of the habits of the fish. Suckers can be handled with almost any kind of rod and line that will allow the fisherman to place his bait where he thinks the fish are resting. Of several things connected with sucker fishing, the angler can be sure, for instance, that if the fish are looking for something to eat, they will be looking for it on the bottom, not in mid-water. So, a sinker is indicated to pull the bait down and keep it down. Second, these fish have small mouths, designed to cope with tiny bits of food. If the suckers run in size from 10 to 15 inches, as our Allegheny fish usually do, a No. 10 hook is the best size. Some anglers use larger hooks, No. 6 or even No. 4, but they do not hook so many fish as they might with smaller hooks.

Bait used is invariably the ordinary garden hackle. Red worms of whatever size turned up by the spade are usable. The bait on the hook should be kept small and compact so a fish can mouth it readily. Two or three tiny worms or a short section of a large one makes a bait possibly one-half an inch long and no more than three-eighths of an inch in diameter. A larger bait will give rise to a long series of tantalizing jerks and nibbles on the line as the fish tears the bait into bits to suit his peculiar anatomy. This business usually ends in a bare, bait less hook for the fisherman. Let him have a small bait on a tiny hook, and he will nearly always hook himself.

This is a very practical method, especially for the angler who is inclined to cat-nap by the fire, or the energetic type who wanders off to hunt Indian relics in a nearby farmer's field, or the nature student absorbed in spying on the mating antics of a pair of wood-ducks up the creek a piece.

Early spring sucker fishing holes are pretty well established. Wherever a small creek flows into a larger one there will be a school of fish. And, at least in Pennsylvania, such places are easily recognizable from the litter left by previous fishermen. But not all the good spots have been discovered. A systematic search by an observant angler may locate a good spot where he can fish in solitude.

The requirements for a good early spring spot are these: A junction of two streams, with a deep pool, a wintering hole, in the largest stream not too far below the junction. The smaller stream does not necessarily need be a fishable one. A tiny brook will have its attraction for the fish whose migratory instinct is beginning to develop. To me, it seems the main requirement is a difference in temperature between the two streams of water. That is, a small stream will warm up sooner, have a quicker reaction to spring sunshine and rain than a larger volume of water.

If, as rarely happens, the small stream is running clear and the bigger stream muddy, a fisherman may have an interesting time watching the fish. Lying quiet on the bank, it is most interesting to observe a school of suckers emerge from the muddy and into the clear water. Then to watch them quarter the bottom searching food, wary as the wild deer, in the clear water. The tiniest shadow will send the fish back into the cloudy water to hide. But watch as one hunts close by the baited hook. He swims partly past, then turns and noses it. A few tentative tasting maneuvers, and then he will quickly bolt the bait. He's caught!

I have a springer spaniel, a woodcock hunter by profession, who accompanies me on most of my sucker fishing excursions. The four canine tusks he possesses make a very effective gaff. He loves it. With a fish on the line, he will stand in the water, watch his chance, and quick as a flash clinch his teeth into the fish's back. Altogether he adds up to the most efficient landing apparatus a fisherman could muster. Only trouble is, his idea of how much dry land should be between the captured fish and the stream is sometimes exaggerated. He thinks there should be plenty. And it is disconcerting to have him come up from the water with a fish in his teeth, then carry it twenty or thirty yards into the bushes before he lays it down. But he has seen fish get away, and he will take no chances with the ones he catches. And as I impatiently untangle my line from the willow bushes, I cannot help but feel that he has the correct approach to the problem of catching fish. Once you have him out of the water, keep him out!

Suckers are, of course, primarily vegetarians, and we may think it odd that worms are so universally used for bait. A little reflection will note that most of the stream bottom vegetation is winter-killed. And that rocky streams are washed clean in the spring-time. This may account for the eagerness with which a sucker bolts the worm bait. Then, too, it may be something similar to the boy who liked such things as candy and dill pickles and ice cream. One at a time, and all was well. But the day he ate them all together, oh my!

CHAPTER 16

Queen of the Water

SOMETIMES IT SEEMS AS if everything moves round in cycles. We have, for instance, the daily rotation of the earth, the migrations of the birds, and the recurring seasons of growth and fruit and frost. Fashions in women's clothing, too, I am told, undergo periodic rebirth. But of all the things associated with our daily life, patterns and fashions in trout flies apparently have escaped this cyclic arrangement.

Down through the years the favorite patterns—the Royal Coachman, the Cahills, the Black Gnat, and many, many others—have appeared each season on the tackle counters and in angler's fly books wholly unchanged. Are trout and trout fishermen so thoroughly bound by tradition they cannot change? I think not.

The business of confining my own fishing to civilized 'fished-out' waters has taught some interesting things. Seeking the crowd instead of the wilderness, fishing for the trout which were able to avoid capture by the hundreds of fishermen who passed before me often demonstrated the need for a better, more life-like fly.

But with all the hundreds of patterns at hand, there is no need to invent a new fly. In fact, it would hardly be possible to put together a combination of colors at the present time that has not at some time in the past been hailed as a real "killer". So, if other things turn up in these recurring cycles, the thought emerges: why not try refurbishing an old trout fly? There can be no harm in it. And I feel sure the original designer, bless his experimental soul, would be whole-heartedly with us in any attempt to modernize his creation.

Without going back over the history of John Wilson's invention, though that is often interesting, it is here sufficient to examine what he has left for us. Could there be a prettier name for a trout fly than Queen of the Waters? Hardly. He gave us a perfect name. And could he have possibly chosen a happier combination of colors to picture all the warmth of a mid-summer sun—the humming insect life of a June day? And tossed in a suggestion of the fragrance of a forest at the height of the summer season, if only to make the cup spill over. A master artist could have done no better, with all his colors.

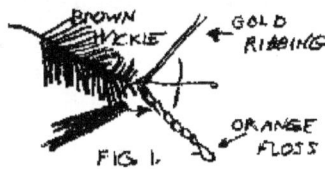

Note the ripe orange of the fly's body, flecks of gold ribbing shining out, the glistening red-brown hackle, and the clear miracle of a mallard feather folded over for a wing. An easy fly to tie, the old pattern; and a durable fly designed for hard fishing. A weedless fly, too, for while ordinarily trout fishermen are not troubled with pond-weeds, the palmer-tied hackle is of tremendous value in salvaging reckless back-casts.

So simple to tie, also—the old fly. And thus, a good one for beginners to practice upon. It goes together in three easy steps. First tie on the brown hackle feather, then the gold ribbing, and then the orange silk floss for the body. In the opposite order, wind them forward over the hook—the floss, the ribbing, and the hackle. Tie each as it is wound in place and lastly fold the pretty mallard feather and tie it in for a wing.

Do you wonder, as you work, why Mother Nature took such infinite pains to print this delicate pattern on each breast-feather of a mallard drake? I do, and I confess I do not know the answer.

We have, here on the Allegheny River at Franklin, Pennsylvania, a flock of mallards who stay with us on the river all winter. They have made their home here in the city for many years and are now quite tame. And they dine royally, through the winter months, on the very best quality of chicken-feed doled out by friendly bird lovers. I never cease to be amused, however, at the vain and proud way the colorful drakes boss their drab ladies around.

Again, on the subject of trout flies, the wet pattern of the Queen of the Waters does well for the beginner to work with, for the palmer hackle will conceal many defects of body taper and uneven ribbing. Too, sometimes it seems as if the more ragged the wet fly appears in the water the more fish it catches, so as a bit of advice to other fly-tiers—always try the fly on the trout no matter how awful it looks to you. But a smooth, graceful body contour is important in a trout fly, as it is in some other forms of art, and well worth striving after.

As to modern flies, the tendency has been toward the hackle and bivisible types, fished dry. If you like a fly to ride the water on tip-toe, then there is no need to fashion wings upon it. And color is of small matter in a high riding fly.

To prove these statements to your own satisfaction, you have only to lie upon the bottom of a trout-stream and let the flies float over you. But, as a word of warning, do not become too completely absorbed in your work. Even if you do not look like a whale, you must, as he does, come up for air every minute or so. Fascinating as this kind of experimentation is, I advise against it, for I am convinced that certain twinges I feel before a storm are connected with some of my youthful excesses in these underwater investigations. The whole trick can be done, and simply, with mirrors.

My principle objection to the hackle flies and the bivisibles is they do not look like much of anything when they are under water. Some fish bite on underwater bivisibles, and some people buy stock in gold mines. Most do neither.

Fishing times are short—the exciting times, that is. The last hour of daylight, or the flurry of madness that grips the trout in the midst of a sudden shower—these are the times a fly fisherman gets in his best licks at big trout. And if his dry fly becomes water-soaked at a time like this, he is more than human if he has the patience to stop fishing and bend on a new fly. The problem is, then, a fly to attract trout whether it floats or sinks, a 'wet-dry' fly, if you please; something that looks edible to a trout the instant he sees it whether he is busy stuffing himself with grasshoppers or shad-flies or pale evening duns.

Thus, we come to the spent-wing fly shown in Fig. 3. The glossy, barred rock wings add the final touch of deception to the fly. Neatly tied, nearly every trout will take it; it seems to fool them completely. Fact is, memory says the majority of big trout took it under water.

The Queen of the Waters is not, we must remember, a fly for opening day. It is a warm weather fly. Its season begins when the first June Bug comes buzzing around the kitchen window. There was one day when the trout were lumpy with June Bugs as they took this 'wet-dry' fly. Another day, and we wondered how the trout had the nerve to strike the golden orange fly, for their sides, were actually distended, packed solidly with grasshoppers. And one never-to-be-forgotten evening when the water swarmed with shad-flies; and every trout took the Queen of the Waters spentwing an inch or so under water as we fished hurriedly in the gathering dusk, too hurriedly to tie on a dry, new fly.

And so, the record goes. Successful conquest of the trout has not been 100 per cent, of course; it never could reach the saturation point and hold there. And I guess we would not want it that way. But the Queen of the Waters is a grand spent-wing 'wet dry' fly; of that we are convinced. We carry size 10 mostly, with a few 8's and 6's where there is some big mouth bass water handy.

And for the bass, do not try to float it on its toes; let its wings stick to the surface of the water so Mr. Bass can feel sure that it will not be able to flit away as he is about to grab it. He is a lazy fellow, mostly. When you think he is eying it, give the fly the gentlest of little twitches, and it is an even chance that what happens next will frighten the dickens out of you!

The dry fly's body is best if made of bright orange wool or fur rather than of silk—it floats better. And our personal preference is for a red rather than a brown hackle. The tail is optional, not called for in the old pattern. We tie it in using a few fibers from the same bird that provided the hackle.

Speaking of birds, our fly now has the advantage of no longer requiring wild bird feathers. A red and barred rock rooster will supply the feathers for nearly a hundred flies. Yearling birds will not do. You want the tough old birds for stiff, glossy feathers.

It should please the bird lovers to know we can make a beautiful and effective trout fly without killing rare birds. And it does, I know, for I like to watch the wild birds myself.

CHAPTER 17

Wrong Way Plugging

Is THE SHOE ON the right foot?

Could a right-handed man do a more efficient job of plug fishing if he used a left-handed casting reel? For instance, could I, a right-handed old dog, learn a new trick? That is, could I learn to use a lefthanded reel?

Scene 1 opens by a placid bass pool along my creek. It is a beautiful afternoon in mid-summer. I sit lazily on the bank as cottony clouds drift across a brilliant sky. It is very still, with the murmuring drone of a million summer insects broken only by the quiet whirrs of a well-oiled casting reel.

An eager young man is methodically covering the pool with his casts. He is a good caster. His plug darts to its mark with the swift precision of a humming bird in full flight.

I study the boy's technique. He is a better caster than I ever hope to be. He's quick as lightning on the retrieve. Then I sit up a little straighter. I see how he works it. He is left-handed. He handles the rod entirely with his left hand; casts, thumbs the reel, and brings the rod tip up and back while his right hand finds the reel handles and winds in the retrieve.

If a straight line is the shortest distance between two points, it is no more direct and to the point than this lad's system of casting and retrieving. He makes no fumbling motions at the finish of each cast, as I do, changing the rod from right to left hand. His reel is never unguarded, even for an instant, as mine is while I shift the rod from hand to hand.

I recall some embarrassing moments in my fishing career, when certain bass, now possessing unprintable nicknames, chose that particular split second to lunge at the bait.

This young fisherman's equipment is orthodox, the same right-hand-drive reel, the same rod and line that nearly all of us use. When he had finished casting the pool, I engaged him in conversation, but briefly.

Yes, he had heard they made left-handed reels for fellows like him, but he had never seen one. He had heard that they were specially made and higher priced, but since he got along O. K. with the standard model, why be fussy? And that is about all the information I got out of him, for then he started pumping me about the fish and the fishing along this creek.

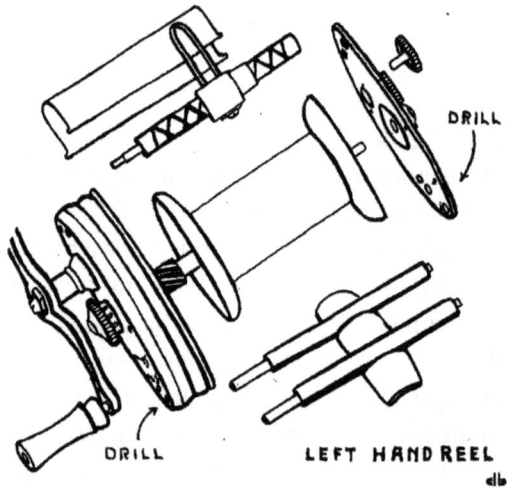

DRILL

DRILL   LEFT HAND REEL

Scene II is in mid-winter, eight months later. Snowflakes are flying, deep drifts block the roads, and the whole landscape is white as snow. So, just when the bass season is at its very lowest ebb, the postman brings a fishing tackle catalogue. And the catalogue is the spark to re-kindle interest in left-handed reels for right-handed fishermen. I decide the only way to put my mind at ease on the subject is to buy a left-handed reel and try to master it next summer.

But there are no left-handed winches listed. I order another catalogue. They don't make one, either. I compose several letters. Nothing develops. Everybody I know is too busy manufacturing standard tackle to make me a left-handed reel for plugging.

A couple of weeks later I am standing by the window. There is still plenty of snow outside, but it is sooty gray and dirty now. Beyond and through the snow I see a water-beaten stump near the lily pads. The silver water shimmers around it as our boat eases silently closer. I cast the tiny plunker, and check it exactly in the shadow of the stump. The water boils. Thumb on silk, I set the hooks. He is a whopper! I crank furiously with my left hand. He is coming up. He jumps!

Boy, what a bass!

I bring the rod around sidewise to throw him off balance and see with the corner of an eye a neighbor woman eyeing me sharply as she visits my wife in the kitchen. I stuff my hands in my pockets, jingle my keys, and step down to the cellar to poke up the furnace!

Scene III shows a cluttered work bench. Small tools and casting reel parts make a jumbled pattern on the bench. But the work proceeds, and there finally emerges from the clutter a serviceable casting reel. The job was not so difficult as I had feared. In fact, I feel sure that any man familiar with the necessary tools could turn out a similar reel provided he wanted one as badly as I did.

The risk was not very great, for I chose a reel that had seen its best days. It was in line for retirement. And if the operation had failed, and the reel gone into the trash can, no great loss would have been incurred.

A standard model was chosen for alteration, one that evidently enjoyed a wide sale before the war. Originally it was intended that exact detail drawings be made to show each step in the alteration, but investigation later showed that this particular reel was made in several different designs, so actual dimensional drawing would perhaps be more confusing than helpful.

Actually, the change-over involved only the marking out and drilling of several new holes in the end plates and a lengthening of the line guide. The unused holes were plugged with small chunks of aluminum, riveted in place. Perhaps the principal danger to guard against in a job like this would be the accidental bending of any of the reel parts as they are held in a vise for drilling.

It is suggested that the reel be dismantled, each part studied, and the necessary alteration mapped carefully before any work is begun. The parts not altered, spool, gears, etc., can be laid by in a little box until the drilling work on the end plates is completed. Note that a bent spool shaft or bearing means a useless reel. The reel pictured is labeled Shakespeare "Criterion" 1960 Model HD.

Scene IV develops naturally. Winter has given way to something resembling spring. I fasten the left-handed reel to a casting rod, remove the hooks from a battered plug for practice purposes, and adjourn to the backyard. But first I check to make sure the aforementioned neighbor lady cannot see me casting for bass in the backyard, as she did in the parlor!

I am a little rusty, of course, but after a few casts my thumb falls into the old groove, and I cast right along. A spaniel puppy comes across lots to investigate, and is very much interested in the old plug as I retrieve it across the lawn.

He is a good substitute for a bass. He pounces on the plug, shakes it viciously, and tries to carry it under the porch. We have a swell workout. I have not the slightest difficulty in winding the reel with my left hand once I get the knack.

As I put up my tackle, I have a feeling that bass season holds some brand new thrills for me this year, and I am impatient for the time to roll around.

Scene V cannot be described until the present season is over. What will happen is hidden in the future. This much I can tell. I have a good right-hand reel laid away just in case of emergency.

CHAPTER 18

Pennsylvania Muskellunge

ESOX MASQLINONGY OHIENSIS is an old native in Allegheny waters. He's been around for a long, long time; and from all indications he intends to remain in the waters of the Allegheny area indefinitely.

From Chautauqua Lake in the north to the mouth of the Clarion River on the lower Allegheny, he can roam about as he pleases, irritated more by polluted waters than by muskie fishermen.

That the fishermen do not irritate him greatly is evident in the fact that every now and then a great fish is found dead along the water. Death came from old age, and not from the hands of the fishermen who pursue him.

The Allegheny itself is a rocky, swiftly-falling stream not exactly suited to fish like muskies. However, it serves as the connecting link between the lakes of the area and the winding weedy streams that tie the whole system together.

It would not do, though, to discount the river as a potential source of muskies, for occasional fish are taken from it. And certainly, more are continually invading its waters in search of food, or adventure, or romance, or whatever it is that muskies search for.

The whole area, including such lakes as Conneaut and Leboeuf, and Sandy Lake, and the flood control lake at Tionesta, is potential muskellunge water. The possibility of hooking a big fish is present almost anywhere in northwestern Pennsylvania.

Let the fisherman beware!

Among those of us who pursue the muskie in western Pennsylvania there is, and probably will continue to be until the end of time, considerable difference of opinion as to the correct method of planning a campaign against him.

Some of us favor live bait, and some favor plugs or spinners. Some are trolling specialists, and others are equally vehement as to the advantages of still fishing. There are men among the muskie fishermen who will spend a whole October day, from dawn to dusk, casting a heavy plug in muskie waters, snatching only a moment to munch a sandwich now and then.

Angling for the prize of all fresh water predatory fishes does something to a man. He knows in the beginning that he may fish for days or even weeks without so much as seeing a fish. He may change his tactics and go from live bait to plugs, and back again, all without success. How, then, is it possible to be in any way helpful to a beginner? How advise a man to best conquer Esox masquinongy ohiensis when the experts are so far from agreement?

Perhaps the only sound advice that can be given is this: Have a stout line on the reel and conspire as best you can to win favor from Lady Luck!

Under the head of live bait, for still fishing or trolling, first in order of popularity is the sucker. Next come outsize minnows and frogs. Little used but with better than average possibilities are small carp and a fish common to the Allegheny, the sandpike or log-perch. I once saw a good fish take a sandpike from the top of the water after he had refused a sucker. These little fish look like miniature walleyed pike, except that they have very tiny mouths. The only way I know of procuring them is by fishing a worm on a very small hook.

Carp minnows do not get the attention they deserve from muskie and bass fishermen in Allegheny waters, probably because they are not so easy to procure as topwater minnows or suckers. It is interesting to note that in New York State the hatchery on Chautauqua Lake provides as food for its muskellunge fry carp minnows raised especially for the purpose. A word to the wise is usually sufficient. Especially when it is noted that all the water in our muskie area abounds in carp.

Before discussing artificial baits in detail, it should be noted that a muskie will strike at almost anything moving in the water—if it appears to be alive. I've experimented and caught small fry, six to ten inches long, with trout flies. But the difference was noted—the little fellow would only lunge at the fly if it were moving swiftly through the water. They would not, like bass, take a fly at rest or gently jiggled somewhere near them.

This is likely the cumulative result of ages of muskellunge history, instinctive and development, if you will, in which the fish learned to catch and kill only clean and healthy food. They are not scavengers, nor are they handicapped in the pursuit of their food as are, for instance, the bass. Streamlined to the nth degree, a muskie is more than a match in speed and precision for any of the food fish he eats.

Another point, and the one that no doubt is responsible in part for the reputation he holds among fishermen, is his absolute fearlessness. When it is considered that muskie of any ordinary size has nothing in the water that he can consider as an enemy, nothing that is able to kill and eat him or even frighten him, the brazen attitude he maintains toward a boatload of fishermen is a little easier to understand. He seems to have absolutely no sense of fear or shyness in the presence of me as do the trout or bass.

While record muskies have been taken on ordinary bass plugs, most dyed-in-the-wool fishermen favor larger lures. And from the variety of shapes and colors such lures, it is evident that no one successful type has yet evolved.

My personal favorite is a large spoon swiftly retrieved; but that fact adds nothing to the sum total of knowledge concerning the subject. It only reveals that my best success has come while casting such a lure. And any success the spoon may have brought can just as easily be attributed to luck as to good judgement.

Large spinners, in connection with bucktail streamers, are widely used as muskie lures. As to the choice of color for any artificial lure, it should be considered that the staple diet of the muskie is almost wholly composed of other fish. The rough fish such as suckers, carp, and various other minnows seem to be the favorites, and, since these are invariably a silvery white below, they indicate a silver or chromimum spinner or spoon blade.

The color of the bucktail is just as much a controversial matter as is the color of the plugs. In line with our thoughts of minnows and suckers, the deer tail should be light in color. White, or pale yellow, or orange tie in best with a nickel or silver spoon or spinner. Many fishermen, however, maintain stoutly that a rich red-brown, like the fur of a pine squirrel, or a dark grey, mouse-colored bucktail is much better than the light, bright colors. Here again is lack of agreement among the experts.

With a fish so cocksure of its ability to catch any fish it wants to eat at any time it chooses, eating must be a very small problem. It is this fact that leads to our belief that luck plays such a large part in any success a muskie fisherman may enjoy.

It must only be the matter of a moment for a muskellunge to decide that it is hungry, catch a fish, and eat it at its leisure. If the fisherman presents his lure at that moment, and it is accepted by the muskie, then the fisherman has placed his foot on the first rung of the ladder of success. Otherwise, he may spend days or even weeks in fruitless fishing until the coincidence of man and hungry muskie occurs again.

Probably the whole answer to the matter of the best bait or lure for muskie fishing lies with the muskie itself, and since it opens its mouth so seldom, it will be a long time before we get the truth of the matter.

In any event, fishing for muskies is probably the top thrill in fresh-water angling. And one of the prize fish of our neighborhood last season, went to a man who stepped down over the river bank, heaved a popping bass plug all of thirty feet out into the Allegheny, and came back up the bank a few minutes later with some eighteen pounds of Esox masquinongy ohiensis struggling in his arms!

CHAPTER 19

Crawdads

WEBSTER DEFINES THE CRAYFISH or craw-fish as a "freshwater lobster-like crustacean." This sort of definition—Willie looks like Joe because Joe looks like Willie, only Joe is bigger—is usually adequate. But in a discussion of the usefulness of crayfish as the supreme live bait for smallmouth bass, our definition ought to be a little more adequate.

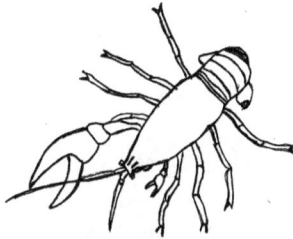

To begin with, Allegheny waters have long been especially rich in varied forms of crustacea. These waters are rich in the minerals shell-building creatures must have; some more than others, of course. Even in the early days, before the development of the oil deposits and the subsequent pollution by waste oils and refinery acids, seepages of Seneca oil (now labeled 100 per cent Pennsylvania oil) and the mineral spring waters were well known to the earliest explorers and settlers.

We are happy to report that, due to more careful refinery practice, plus utilization of what were formerly considered as waste oils, the Allegheny River is considerably cleaner than it was twenty years ago. And with the consummation of Governor Duff's pollution program, the river will once again be in condition to provide the best of smallmouth bass fishing to thousands of happy tourists.

The crayfish is a hardy fellow in some ways, and again he is delicate and easily destroyed. He grows, as every fisherman knows, by casting off his old shell after he has grown a new one a size larger underneath it. This may sound like an impossible trick, to grow a new and bigger shell beneath the old one, but it is done simply by keeping the new shell soft and pliable until after the old one is discarded. It is at this changing time that he is most vulnerable.

The actual process of shedding the old shell is usually done at night, probably for reasons of security. It normally requires only about five to ten minutes. As soon as the new shell is exposed it begins to harden, a process that seems to depend on the water temperature. In warm water it will be completely hard in a day or so, while in a cold brook it may take several times as long.

Some local fishermen noticed this and have taken to storing their soft live bait in mechanical refrigerators. My old friend, Charlie, used to do this. He did it, that is, until the time he and his wife went away for a vacation. She turned the machine off—and he forgot the can of "crabs" he had stored away inside. Of course, they died; and when she opened the refrigerator door two weeks later, she immediately laid out some new rules as to who should put what in her icebox!

For bass bait, the crayfish are used when they are about ready to shed, when the shell has been newly shed, and also after they have begun to harden. We boys along the river called them "peelers," "mushers," and "paper-backs."

In all the years we have fished with them we never noticed any preference on the part of the bass for either type.

Where crayfish are plentiful along the water the experienced man will rarely catch a hard-shelled one. He can judge from its color whether or not it will be usable. To an amateur this is very confusing. There seem to be as many colors or shades as there are crustaceans. And where one "paperback" may be blue-gray the next one may be red or tan.

"Peelers" are uniformly dark in color and may be distinguished by the tell-tale red that shows around the tips of the claws, the toes, and the fringe at the tip of the tail. Freshly peeled or very soft crayfish are quite beautiful, with an iridescent sheen on the back and a clean ivory underneath. But only the experienced eye can pick out the good ones either in daylight or at night with the aid of a flashlight.

Like a lot of other tricks, catching soft-shelled crayfish is best learned by practice.

Where he lives undisturbed in the water the crayfish is a solitary creature. Each one makes his own home under a stone—or by digging a burrow in the clay. He spends a lot of time fixing this den to suit, and in keeping it neat and clean. When the time comes to change coats, he moves into shallow water and hides under any convenient weed or stone. And he stays in the shallows until his new coat is completely hardened before venturing back into deep water.

This is possibly the only way he can avoid his water-borne enemies, but there are a lot of land creatures who like to feast on him at this time—crows, blackbirds, ducks, raccoons and opossums—to name a few. And not to mention Man, the only predator of the lot who will take more than he can use.

To keep two or three dozen soft-shell crayfish alive for several days is a difficult task. Chemically treated tap water in variably kills them overnight. If closely confined in a bait pail, they will fight and murder one another.

A basket filled with damp water weeds or grass, with plenty of room for the crab to hide from one another, is good. And if ice can be added now and then to keep things cool and moist, they will stay lively for several days.

Along this same line, a very successful method is to roll each crayfish in a foot square section of newspaper and fold over the ends so as to make a snug dark little compartment for him. Place these in a basket, sprinkle with enough water to moisten the paper, and drape a moistened burlap sack around the basket. Kept moist the crayfish can live for three or four days without refrigeration or fresh water.

However, if you have to keep them several days, don't take the "peelers" or the "mushers," for they will nearly always die. And the odor of a crayfish—dead only an hour on a summer afternoon—is, as Charlie's wife found out, and the bobbysoxers say—"out of this world".

Not a few writers have suggested that the crayfish is the favorite or staple food of the small-mouthed bass. This we do not believe, though we do think that a soft-shelled "crawdad" is the best live bait that can be used to entice him.

Because the crayfish come into the very shallowest water to shed their old shells, and are careful to remain in the shallows until the new ones are completely hard, the odds are all against the bass catching them at this time.

True, Mr. Bass may get an occasional one that has been chased out by some creature prowling the shoreline—or one who was foolish enough to choose the edge of a deep pool for his dressing-room. These rare tidbits he may get are most likely the reason for his eagerness to grab one impaled upon a fish hook.

The popular fallacy has probably developed because so many bass contain remnants of crayfish when they are killed. Many thousands of words have been penned praising the fighting heart of the small-mouthed bass, but still the story of his gameness has not been completely told. And probably never can be finished, for he will never quit fighting.

The first thing a bass does when he finds he is in for a battle is to disgorge the contents of his stomach. Empty, he fights better. But since he eats hard-shelled crayfish when other food is not readily available, he may have the remains of one of these in his tummy, and this he cannot get rid of so easily. The pointed claws and legs cannot be disgorged as readily as the soft remains of minnows.

We suggest that the next time a bass is cleaned it be noted that the crayfish in his stomach was a hard-shelled one. Also, to watch closely the next few bass hooked in clear water, and see if they do not attempt to get rid of whatever they had previously eaten.

It matters not whether we hook a hefty small-mouth on artificial bait, or fool him with a lively soft-shelled crayfish. When we do, we are in for a fight to the end.

CHAPTER 20

Carp—Our Problem Child

SOMETIMES IT SEEMS, LOOKING over various fishing waters, that the carp are by far the most abundant fish we have to show for all our conservation efforts.

Wherever the water is at all suitable, the carp have made themselves completely comfortable. They have long since settled down to raise their multitudinous families.

Many fishermen have condemned carp as a nuisance and as a threat to our fishing and called them many other things too numerous to list in an article of this kind. I recollect one gentleman, evidently in training for political office, who described the carp as a "despicable interloper, spawned in the filth of the Orient and foisted upon us in the guise of" and so on and on in a deep bass voice.

I might have pointed out to him that some of our own rivers are equally as filthy as any in the Far East, at least I am told they are by boys who have seen both. But naturally, I did not think of it until after I had walked away. Besides, he had worked his blood pressure up to the pink all by himself, and with no prodding from me.

Carp were first brought to America in 1877. That is three generations of men, or 70 years, ago. Those first imported carp were valuable. A hatchery was established, and two specially designed railway cars built to distribute the young fish. These were doled out, twenty fish to each farmer who made application and who had fulfilled the requirement of establishing a suitable pond to receive them.

Some ponds were flooded out, and thus the fish escaped. So far as we know, no large-scale effort was ever made to stock public fishing waters. Whether these fish were distributed in large numbers or not, back there in the gay nineties is of no consequence now. The carp are with us and plenty of 'em.

The original reason behind the carp importation may not be clearly understood by some younger readers. In fact, conversation has shown that many belonging to the second generation have not clearly understood the original thinking that brought the carp over here from Europe.

Records show that inland fish ponds had been carefully tended in European countries for centuries. We must recollect that railroads were nonexistent, even in Europe, a long time ago. Transportation was slow, very expensive, and refrigeration practically unknown. Yet these people, dim as their knowledge of nutrition must have been, recognized a need for fresh fish as part of their diet.

Because it was impossible to transport fresh seafood more than a very few miles inland in summer time, they turned to their own waters for fish. Hence, a natural gravitation to ponds where the fish could be more easily controlled.

Fish ponds and fish culture reached a high state of development in some parts of Europe and the British Isles in those early centuries. A little imagination permits us to visualize the county fairs and market days of those ancient times, with the sturdy farm folk pridefully exhibiting their carefully bred and pond-raised fish, much as we in our time gather to admire the best in beef cattle and poultry.

The carp were a cash crop, just as the goose feathers and the fat roosters were cash or trading stock. So, these fish were valuable, as a necessary addition to the diet of the people of the times.

What more natural reaction, then, among our forefathers, than to establish farm fish ponds in a raw new country where distances were great and transportation more difficult than in civilized Europe? We can almost hear these men telling their sons about grandfather's pond back in Austria or in Wales, and describing the fat juicy fish that grew in it.

But the railroads came, the ponds were forgotten, and now look at the carp in our country. Someone has described the United States as a melting pot, and so far as the human race is concerned that seems to be gradually coming true. But where lesser creatures are concerned no such mingling occurs. A starling begets a starling, and sparrows remain sparrows through unnumbered generations.

They may adapt themselves to new conditions, as the sparrows have learned to descend upon an automobile when it is parked at the curb, picking off the choicest, nicely toasted insects imbedded in the radiator screen. I wonder what they will turn to next, when all the cars are new, with the radiators concealed under a labyrinth of chromium bars?

The carp is quite as adaptable a fellow as the English sparrow. If there is meat to eat, he will eat it. And if there is no meat, larvae or crustacea, that is, he will turn to and graze, depending on herbage for his sustenance. And if the underwater grazing is not to his liking, he will come up and munch upon the plants that grow on dry land! This we have seen him do, honestly!

Our problem is not, however, an investigation into his queer habits but, rather, to figure out how we can best make use of him. For one experiment, we suggest that specimens of the Great Pike, Esox lucius, be imported from European waters where they have been living with the carp for a long, long time. These fish must have learned a long time ago to depend upon the carp minnows for sustenance.

And what a few hundred of them might do to the carp population of a small American lake would be interesting to study. Perhaps we could, in time, and in controlled hatchery ponds, develop a strain of black bass who would prefer carp minnows to any other wild food. With no intent to label either a small mouth or a large mouth a thief, here is a good place to ring in the old saying "set a thief to catch a thief."

All this would require considerable time and study. For a quick return on our present carp surplus, we propose that an immediate incentive be supplied to stimulate fishing for 'em.

For instance, there are several fishing contests sponsored by different interests throughout our country, with prizes for the biggest trout, bass, muskie, etc. Why not a contest for carp? Would it be disgraceful to win a prize for landing a thirty or a forty-pound carp? He may be a minnow to a student of ichthyology, but he is no minnow on the end of a fishing line! We'll guarantee that one!

Not many such carp will be landed with ordinary bass tackle, if our own experience proves anything. Here we may be accused of hiding an ulterior motive, for these big carp have cost us many fishing lines and not a few broken bass rods.

We used to fish the lower Allegheny for small-mouthed bass, with soft-shelled crayfish bait. Once in a while a big carp would pick up the bait and head either downstream toward Pittsburgh or upstream in the general direction of Salamanca, N. Y. The result was inevitable with our bass tackle—something broke!

We would like to kill one of those fish, but we have no incentive except revenge. If there was a chance of winning a silver loving cup inscribed "To the best carp fisherman in the whole United States of America—Year 1948 A.D.", we'd get some surf fishing tackle and three or four hundred yards of nine thread line and go after him. And we'd have a lot of competition.

Lastly, there is always the question of utilizing carp as human food. Tastes differ. Some people like carp, and some are so prejudiced against the name that they will not even taste it knowingly. In the eight or ten years we have been investigating, we have tried to keep an open mind on the whole subject. We have fried carp from every different kind of water where we caught them, and the whole subject is confusing.

Some carp are good to eat, some are not, and there seems to be no way this can be explained. Some carp from stagnant pot holes were sweetly edible, while others from clean pure water, after one taste, went to feed the chickens.

After a long study of the matter we have no definite answer. The only way to find out whether the carp from any fishing water are good to eat is fry 'em and try 'em.

One part we always save, though, is the roe. No matter where we caught the carp, we saved the roe when we found it, and it was always good to eat. Suppose you try some.

CHAPTER 21

Fly Rod Frequency

A GREAT DEAL HAS been written on the subject of choosing a suitable fly rod. Without discounting previous literature on the subject, the purpose here is to outline a method for quickly determining the usefulness of such a fishing rod; and further, to reveal some of the flaws that creep into rod production to cause later dissatisfaction and sometimes failure.

Offhand, there seems to be little in common between a fly rod and a violin, or a piano string. But they do have one thing in common, and that is a natural period or frequency of vibration. Every fly rod has a natural vibratory frequency acquired in the course of its construction. Unlike the violin string or the piano wire, it is not subject to change, or tuning, once the rod is built, wrapped, and varnished.

This natural period of vibration, while not used in ordinary fishing or casting motions, nevertheless determines the speed, the "action," and the power of any rod to perform any given trick. A rod's natural vibratory time determines whether it has a "dry fly" or a "wet fly" action. It also determines the length and weight of line it will safely handle.

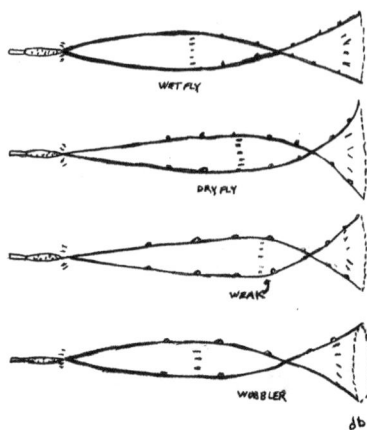

With this connection in mind, and a little study of the subject; it be-comes possible to choose a rod from the dealer's stock, and without actually casting, to be assured that the chosen rod will perform as expected.

The advantages in learning to choose a rod in this manner are twofold. First, very few dealers provide space for rod trial. Most stores have not the space.

Second, and more important, vibrating the rod at its natural period will show hidden defects that may not be noticed in actual casting, but which will surely shorten the useful life of the rod. The process is ridicu-lously simple. Only the observations require study and contemplation. Set the rod vibrating as in the diagrams. Study the curves and the nodes. Elec-trically we call them standing waves, and sometimes some other things; but the point here is to carefully observe the curves as the vibration is sustained by the hand.

The diagrams show the different types of rod action. A sharp eye, and a certain amount of experience, will permit any man to judge the stiffness, strength, or weakness of a fly rod in a moment.

Defects, as a weak spot or an unsymmetrical curve, will stand out clearly as the rod vibrates. Unsymmetrical curves are never beautiful, whether they are observed along a bathing beach or a trout brook. And any departure from smoothly flowing curves, perhaps more especially in a fly rod, is a danger sign—a sign of hidden weakness.

A ferrule with only the slightest degree of looseness will telegraph its message plainly to the hand. And with ferrules it is best to catch the first sign of looseness and repair them. To wait until the rod falls apart, or the water seeps into the bamboo, is only begging for trouble.

In the case of a three-piece rod, it is sometimes difficult to be sure which joint is at fault, if only slightly loose. The offending one can be proven by the process of elimination. Remove the butt joint and vibrate the tip and middle sections. If the feeling of wobble is no longer present, then it is elementary that the trouble must have been in the first joint.

This vibration test will condemn a good many rods that have the tendency to depart from a single plane of vibration and assume a rotary motion. This can be controlled to some extent by the hand. However, a rod with a clear inclination to drive its tip in a rotary or oval oscillation is to be suspected. It may perform passably with a heavier than usual line, but since its action shows that it sets up unequal stresses in the wood, it naturally follows that something is liable to give way someday. Some rods of this nature can be made serviceable, though, by careful realignment and wrapping the guides along a plane that shows the minimum of circular wave motion.

Good tools and complete knowledge of their uses and their limitations are the marks of a skilled craftsman. The possibility of becoming a skilled fly fisherman is limited by many, many things. Muscular coordination, keen eyesight, and general health can be developed by following in Izaac's footsteps. For a final successful completion of the project, however, a thorough knowledge of his fly rod is as necessary to the angler as is the knowing where to spade the earth for angle worms during a prolonged drought.

CHAPTER 22

Curiosity

THE POINT IN QUESTION is not exactly the description of interesting things that occur in the woods and fields; those events that make fishing such a fascinating hobby. Rather it is an investigation into the mental processes of various wild creatures in an attempt to determine whether any of their actions are prompted by curiosity, as we understand the word.

Not too much has been written concerning the exhibition of curiosity by our more common game animals. Charles Darwin describes an experiment of his at the zoo. He had a stuffed snake which he placed in a small box with a hinged lid attached. He put the box on the floor of the monkey cage. One animal, of course, lifted the lid, saw the snake, let out a horrified shriek—and departed! Whereupon all the others, each in his turn, were drawn by a morbid curiosity to lift the lid of the box and risk a peek.

Probably the reason I remember Darwin's experiment so clearly is because it so nearly paralleled my own boyish experience. I took a small green snake to school one day, in my pocket. It was no novelty to the boys, naturally; but each little girl in turn seemed drawn by some horrible fascination until she had to ask to see the snake, and when she saw it to shriek and jump away. This is told with no intent to belittle the ladies, whose real courage, I find, surpasses that of most men. But we ought to get down to cases, to see if we can definitely establish any facts about the curiosity of wild animals.

A fox trapper I know relies on suspicion for his most successful operations. He sets a trap in the top of a stump or in an ant hill, forgets it until he figures the man scent is gone; then walks past one day and drops a dead chicken nearby on the ground. He figures that the fox will be suspicious of a dead chicken deep in the woods and far from any henhouse. Also, that the fox, although suspicious of the chicken and the man's tracks and scent, will be drawn by curiosity. The stump or hummock concealing the trap provides a neat vantage point for Mr. Fox to inspect the situation. And thus, the suspicious and finally curious fox is caught.

His set has also an advantage in that unwanted animals—skunks, opossums, raccoons, or hunting dogs—hardly ever get hurt. They usually go directly to the bait, not being so suspicious.

But even with so clever an arrangement as this, not all foxes are caught. He told me about one fox that came nightly to the chicken, but would not approach it closely or jump up on the stump and into the trap. Finally, and at loss about what to do without disturbing his set, he peeled all the bark from a sapling about twenty feet from the stump, on the other side, away from the chicken.

With two suspicious items to examine, sly Renard's curiosity got the better of him, and he hopped up on the stump to investigate the new situation. He stayed right there until next morning!

The fox has a reputation for being a highly intelligent creature. So, for that matter, has the beaver. And beavers are quite common in our part of Pennsylvania. I like to think of beavers as being more headstrong than clever. No matter how many times you destroy the dam he builds in an unwanted location, he will doggedly rebuild it. Flooding a highway or a drainage ditch is no concern of his.

One big beaver moved into a little secret pond of mine. It held besides the usual stock of turtles, frogs, bullheads, and sunfish, a notable family of big-mouth bass. They were the principle attraction; and I visited the pond several times each bass season.

After the beaver moved in (I guessed it was an old male) fishing became almost hopeless. Just about the time in late afternoon for the fish to begin to feed the beaver would come out, swim around, and scare the daylights out of them.

I tried to frighten the beaver into hiding, but it was no use. He just wasn't scared of me. Finally, one day I had an inspiration. I'd take the dog along. He would scare the beaver, and after a little while we could fish in peace.

We reached the pond, I rigged my tackle, the beaver came out to cruise around as usual, and the dog spied him. Pell-mell into the water after the beaver went the dog. I chuckled in high glee. He, the dog, was a springer spaniel about three years old.

Both animals were about the same size. But the beaver wasn't scared, as I had hoped. When the dog would swim within ten feet of him the beaver would dive, "ker-whack", and reappear a moment later twenty yards away.

Which animal, dog or beaver, exhibited the most curiosity concerning the other would be hard to say. Certainly, neither showed fear—only curiosity. And, needless to explain, no bass were caught during the swimming and diving exhibition that followed. Finally, the spaniel quit. He was exhausted. And many times, in the years since that day, I have watched him sit on the bank as beavers swam close by—he only mildly interested. Whether his curiosity was completely satisfied that afternoon, or whether he is fully convinced that he can't catch 'em anyhow, we will never know. But he is now content to let them pass unmolested.

And just to point out how easy it is to be mistaken, the old 'dog' beaver proudly displayed two cute 'pups' the next summer. They still live in the pond and so, too, do the bass.

I have not caught any!

Freshwater bass, I believe, exhibit a good deal of curiosity. Anyone who has fished in clear water has seen the bass rush toward a commotion in the water, then stop at a respectable distance to size up the situation.

Of course, an ichthyologist will say that any fish is a pin-head insofar as brains are concerned. And one who has killed and dissected a small-mouth bass will readily admit that his brain is positively puny alongside that of an old buck deer's, for instance. But then, there are other people who maintain that an ant is a highly intelligent creature; yet his brain is infinitesimal compared with that of a two-pound black bass.

I've seen bass do things I thought were pretty smart. Item: One day I was sneaking along a good-sized trout brook, the water low and very clear. I tip-toed toward the tail of a good pool, hoping to spot a trout. I saw, instead, the tail of a bass fanning below a little snag near the shore.

And just about the time I saw him he suspicioned something and scooted upstream into deeper water. I stood my ground; and in a few minutes I saw him cruising down toward me. But he stopped about fifty feet distant, and after a quick look returned to the deep pool. I was standing in the clear, in an open pasture field possibly four feet above the water level.

I have no doubt that he recognized me for what I was—a fisherman. Curious (just like any other wild creature), I thought I would experiment a little and find out how good his vision really was. I moved back about ten feet and waited quietly. Pretty soon he came down, spied me, and returned to the depths. I backed up again; he saw me again. By this time, we were seventy-five feet apart. I could hardly bring myself to believe that he was actually seeing me, but he certainly acted as if he was suspicious. This might have continued all day, but by this time I was determined to stick it out with him, so I moved farther down the creek bank. But about this time complications entered the set-up. A sleek Jersey cow wandered up to the brook between the bass and me. The bass turned and looked toward the cow, then swam sedately down and took up his former position under the snag!

Your guess is as good as mine!

Did the cow's presence make the bass forget about me, or had I finally retreated so that he could no longer distinguish me? I was, by that time, nearly a hundred feet away. And how does a bass learn that a cow means him no harm, and a man usually comes equipped with malice aforethought? Or was the bass merely curious about my movements and lost interest in them when the cow came along?

All of which adds up to little more than nothing, mentally. But it does prove that a bass can recognize a man a long way under ideal conditions and is suspicious or curious about him.

Now a deer has a lot bigger brain than a bass, that is obvious. I spent a good many seasons hunting deer in Central Pennsylvania. Up there are mountains and upland plateaus several miles off the beaten path and deer who never see a man from one hunting season until the next. In my opinion these deer are easy to shoot. Some will stand and look and let you walk right up to within a hundred yards of them.

But in the oil country, in Western Pennsylvania, the deer have a much higher education. They know what the score is. And though you see them often in the spring and summer months, they showing no signs of being unduly alarmed by your presence; when the shooting starts, they become very shy indeed.

Any deer has two strikes on a hunter when the hunting game begins. The deer's powers of scent and hearing are very much more acute than the man's. To even things, a deer is noticeably near-sighted compared to the average man. In wooded country, coupled with the deer's camouflage coat, it all adds up to a sporting proposition with the odds in favor of neither the hunter nor the hunted. Chance usually picks the winner.

And if the younger bucks of the backwoods country are innocent enough to stand and watch curiously as a man approaches, even the smallest fawns in the oil region seem to know that a man with a gun is dangerous.

If any one statement could be made regarding the over-all intelligence of deer it could be this: the more they know about man (the hunter) the more liable they are to circle around him and sneak away, rather than flee directly in front of him. In other words, the more bitter experience the deer have had with men the less curiosity they will show concerning them.

I fell asleep one afternoon in the deer season. It was a bright, warm day in December. A windless, drowsy day—even the jays were quiet. I must have slept for a couple of hours, for when I awoke the sun was low, near the horizon, and all its warmth was gone.

I had sprawled on the dry, curly white-top grass of a little clearing five miles from any usable highway. And when I awoke, lazily, the first things I saw were a doe and her two fawns.

They stood watching me, not more than twenty or thirty feet away!

Exhibiting remarkable presence of mind (for me) I lay quiet and watched them. And they watched me. The fawns were most active. They pranced around—now close, now jumping away. Mama stayed at a more respectable distance. She more or less divided her attention between me and the surrounding forest. Every now and then one of the fawns would stomp. I suppose it was the stomping that awakened me, though I cannot remember.

But curiosity was evident in every movement of the three deer. This was certainly something new to them—a man sound asleep in the middle of the forest. I have often wondered how long it took them to work up the courage to come so near to me. And I also wonder what first aroused their curiosity. Was it scent or sight or sound?

Like most men, I always maintained that I slept silently—didn't snore! Then I bought one of those home-recording machines. The first things my wife did, after she learned how to run it, was to capture a recording of my sleeping noises. The record is irrefutable evidence that I do snore—and magnificently!

No wonder the fawns were curious. Now that I have heard myself, as it were, I can understand their perplexity!

I remember another doe, under different circumstances, though I think she was more worried than curious.

A dozen of us ganged up to drive a thick piece of deer cover. After a short council of war, we agreed that it would be practically impossible to drive the deer out, so we decided to scatter the watchers at random in the brush, let the drivers circle around a time or two, and get the deer on their feet and keep them moving. I drew a watching position.

Visibility was nearly zero in this young red-oak country, so a few minutes after the others of the crew went on, I climbed a tree. I got about ten feet off the ground, found a horizontal limb, and sat on it

A moment later a big doe came mincing out of the bushes, stepping carefully on the dry leaves, and stopped exactly beneath me, under the tree. She looked back; and I could still hear, faintly, the voices of my companions moving away.

She listened carefully and sniffed at my tracks around the tree trunk. She was plainly nervous but careful to make no sound when she moved about.

She evidently sensed I was nearby, but she didn't know where, so she stayed right under my tree. Finally, after ten or twelve minutes, I became convinced no buck was following her, so I started teasing her. I spat quietly on her rump. She whirled her head, sniffed the tobacco juice, and snorted.

I've fed tame deer tobacco, which they ate with apparent relish. She was not tame, evidently, for it really worried her! I spat several times more, and she didn't like it; but she didn't know what to do about it so she stayed under the tree. Eventually I tired of all this, so I carefully aimed my cap and dropped it. It landed squarely on her left ear. She left the country! She would have taken the cap with her, I think, if it had not fallen off on the second jump.

The sudden ending of my trail-scent at the base of the tree evidently baffled her, as did the spray of tobacco juice, but she never thought to look up in the tree.

I cannot recommend tree climbing in deer country. In Pennsylvania you feel much more comfortable hid behind a great big rock!

When you add it all up, the raccoons are likely the most inquisitive wild creatures of them all. It would be easy to fill a book with their maneuvers. The things they will investigate are innumerable.

But the saddest 'coon I ever saw, was the one that got its fingers caught in a good big fresh water clam. It was in one awful fix. And though it was supposed to be tame, a pet, it took the combined efforts of three of us to unsnarl it from the clam!

This subject of wildlife curiosity is fascinating, and, of course, endless. You need no open season to pursue it. And, looking back, most of the wild animals I have met here in the oil country have shown very little curiosity concerning people; because, I suppose, they are familiar with people.

Perhaps it is this lack of the rubbernecking habit on the part of the woods-dwellers hereabouts that endears them to me.

CHAPTER 23

Pat and Mike
and the Rainbow Trout

You TAKE A COUPLE of men named Pat and Mike, add four cans of rainbow trout fingerlings, and you have the basis of a good fish story.

Only this is not exactly a story in the accepted Pat and Mike vein. This one happens to be true. Pat and Mike have finally started something practical, I think.

Deward Wykoff (nicknamed Pat) and Mike Donley live in north central Pennsylvania. They are members of that vast sportsmen's club, the Clinton County Fish and Game Association. Among other things, the club maintains a pond in the Kettle Creek country where they receive newly hatched trout fry in the spring, feed 'em all summer, and release them in the fall.

A year ago, Pat and Mike drew an assignment from the club to help distribute these fingerlings. With a good day's work behind them they drew four cans of rainbow fingerlings to restock the brook nearest their homes.

It's a quarter mile carry over rough country to the headwaters of their brook. And after they had lugged the first two cans in, and raced uphill to the car, the whole thing began to be hard work, no less.

About that time Pat says to Mike, or Mike says to Pat (it isn't clear who weakened first),"Let's put 'em in the beaver pond." Put to a vote, the decision was unanimous, neither party dissenting. Since the beaver pond is right beside the road; within spitting distance, that is, it doubtless influenced the voting.

This particular pond is about as small as they come, 40 or 50 feet wide, maybe a hundred feet long, and possibly four to five feet deep near the dam. It is 10 or 12 years old, and contains, always, an over-abundant population of four to five-inch brook trout plus a few wise old lunkers. It gets a hard going over by tourist and native fishermen each season. Many of these small trout are caught over and over again, unless they swallow the hook, of course. Anyway, Pat and Mike dumped the remaining 200 three to five-inch rainbow fingerlings into the beaver pond and hurried home to supper.

Next June is where I come in. Pat and Mike told me about the rainbows they had stocked in the brook and, after a little "hemming and hawing," about the ones they had dumped into the pond.

Frankly, they were a bit worried. Several fishing trips to the pond in April and in May had netted as many baby brook trout as usual, but nary a single rainbow had turned up.

They thought they might have died. And felt a little guilty for, as Pat put it, wasting them.

We visited the pond, and proceeded to fish. After a while, I hit the combination and unlocked the door to Pat's and Mike's rainbows. And they were beautiful.

Mind you, the season had been open for six or seven weeks. Dozens of fishermen had tried the water and caught brookies only. But the other trout were there, fat and incredibly sassy, if you knew the combination.

As we caught the rainbows, we measured them before we let 'em loose. They had grown, in one winter, to an amazingly uniform eight inches. This the more remarkable because the pond is, as always, over-populated with small brook trout. We caught five-inch brook trout that day with no sign of parr markings, but the eight-inch rainbows had 'em.

The insect trout food supply of a new made beaver pond is tremendous, but after a few years it tapers off as fertility of the bottom soil changes, and as the weight of trout increases.

I think the reason the boys' rainbows grew so much faster than the native brook trout was because the rainbows went after a totally different class of insects—food the brook trout ignored. Don't hold me to this, it's just a guess.

I do know that a small brook trout will go all out to catch a dry fly the size of a bumblebee, and a small rainbow will lunge just as viciously after a fly no bigger than a flea off your hound dog—or mine. Mine has fleas, I know. Thus, the rainbows waxed fat and colorful while the brookies found slim pickings in the old beaver pond.

We have, in Pennsylvania, dozens of these beaver ponds, with the same stunted brook trout population. Other states have them, I feel sure. If 20 rainbow fingerlings can be added to a small pond 50 by 100 feet (less than a quarter of an acre) and grow to legal sized fish over winter, it's something of a low-cost miracle, and worth a try in other ponds and in other sections of the country. Little ponds can get pretty warm in midsummer, and the question will arise—can the rainbows take a brown stagnant beaver pond which isn't very pleasant to look at along in late summer, but in many of the ponds I know the brook trout survive, so am not worried about the rainbows. We are told they can stand warmer water than can brook trout.

But just to check up on this I drove back to the pond on the last day of our trout season, which is the last day of July. I caught trout in the stagnant, coffee colored water, both brook and rainbow, though not as many as I had two months before. But then I did not fish as vigorously, or as long, for the sun was beastly hot and the mosquitos fierce. If these rainbows survive the summer, as I have every reason to believe they will, from catching them on July 31—what comes next? As they grow, they will begin to forsake their microscopic insect diet and look for solid food. They will see hundreds of small brook trout and my guess is, they will eat 'em. And if they do, we will have some real tackle busters on our hands some of these days. For that happy climax, we will just have to wait and hope.

If this pleasant prospect should materialize, we will have in these small ponds, a situation somewhat akin to that of the southern bass-bream combination, excepting only that the rainbows will be, most likely, unable to spawn.

It seems to me that Pat and Mike made a substantial contribution to the science of trout culture the day they ran out of breath.

CHAPTER 24

Weedless Bass Bug

HERE AND THERE AMONG the weeds of Pennsylvania's lakes and ponds hang various cork bodied bass bugs. No doubt some belong to other anglers; but by times it seems as if we lost 'em all.

Not only are the lost bugs gone but a great many good fish have been scared by the queer antics of a man trying to retrieve a bug. Too, there has been from time to time a considerable, and in the light of present knowledge, wholly unnecessary expenditure of energy in this direction. Energy that, as Charlie says might better be expended scaling fish.

Cork bodied bass bugs, like horseless carriages, are undoubtedly here to stay. Unfortunately, if a cork bug is to be a good fish getter it needs a wide mouthed hook, plenty of clearance between body and barb. This of course is exactly what is needed to catch the most weeds.

So, when the bass fishing fever strikes, you buy or make a bug according to these specifications, hasten to the nearest pond or lake and you fish around in open water until a big bass crashes back in amongst the weeds. And there you go. Pretty soon you are back at the counter or at your workbench choosing or whittling a new bug. There may be a lake somewhere where big bass cruise in clean open water while the little fellows splash in the weedy sections. If such a lake exists, I know it not; and I doubt that it is fished by mortal men.

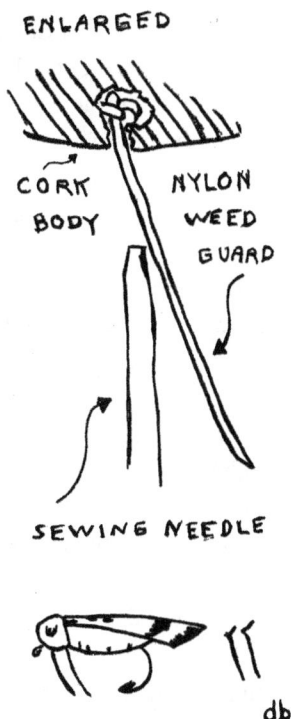

ENLARGED

CORK BODY

NYLON WEED GUARD

SEWING NEEDLE

db

All of which leads us to a description of a successful application of the weedguard principle to a cork bodied bass bug. They say necessity is the mother of invention, and in that respect, I am willing to confess this little novelty was born of desperation. When you are hip deep in muck and water, surrounded by bass and spatterdocks, you're desperate!

The drawing shows the method of attaching the weed guards to a cork bug. The guards are made of nylon leader, of a strength proportional to the weight of the whole lure. For a small bug on a No. 8 hook use six-pound nylon. Heavier bugs want heavier leader material in the weed guards. By tying the knot as illustrated the weed guards are securely anchored inside the cork body without the necessity for cementing or tying them in place. They will stay put if there is life in the cork. Use a heavy needle to press home the knotted ends. It works better with the point broken off.

After you have fixed up some bugs with these weed guards, I suggest you use a heavy leader. Eight or even ten-pound stuff is not too light. In the first place, though you will find your weedless bug slips through most top water weeds easily, it is still possible to get hung up. The guards are not 100% effective. However, the snags are not usually so firm as with the unguarded hook. A slow steady pull will ordinarily free the lure with a minimum of commotion. Perhaps the nicety of bigmouth bass fishing lies in making just enough commotion to attract the fish, without scaring him. A rugged leader will get your lure out of some places where you would be sure to frighten the fish if you had to go get your lure.

Secondly, when you hook a fish in these surroundings you don't get the ripping, splashing battle you expect in open water. Usually Sir Bigmouth throws a couple of half hitches around a mess of weed stems and hangs up helpless. He does, that is, if your leader can stand the strain. Not that it must be strong enough to hold the dead weight of the fish. There is a resiliency in the tangled weeds that stops him from getting a solid pull. I would wager a ten-pound bass cannot break a ten-pound leader by snarling it in the spatterdocks or lily stems. Though I hasten to relate, somewhat sadly, I have not yet had that glorious situation arise.

Once he has done with his tangling it is your move to pick him out. If he is a two-hand bass, that is, if he is big enough to make you drop your rod and grab with both hands, he is a dandy, and I am glad you got him.

We have long since reached the conclusion that picking two hand bass is a lot more fun than picking watermelons. Fix up a weedless bass bug and get in there after them.

CHAPTER 25

Weeds or Fish

IT MAY SEEM A far cry from a vigorous stand of hybrid corn to a small fish pond, but a comparison is possible, and I think we ought to consider it.

In the first place, corn just doesn't "grow". A good crop is the end result of careful planning, choice of seed, soil preparation, fertilization, cultivation, weed control, sun, sweat, and prayer. Some of the best brains in America are dedicated to growing corn. And from the 15 or 20 bushels of grandfather's time to present bumper crops has been a tremendous stride in "know-how". Bear well in mind the men responsible are by no means satisfied. Their goal is 300 bushels to an acre. It all depends on the knowledge born of experience, and the will to keep trying.

I do not mean to say that our thinking on the subject of small fish ponds has been entirely stalled in the ruts of horse and buggy days. We have made some gains in knowledge. We have had it shown that fertilization will substantially increase a fish crop. That weeds are as detrimental to good fishing as they are detrimental to good corn production is, I think, elemental. But have we investigated fully such angles as choice of seed, cultivation, crop rotation cycles, hybrid vigor, and possibly other items connected with small pond fish growth?

Take the case of beavers, and beaver ponds and native brook trout, for instance. Beavers have shown us here in Pennsylvania that vigorous fish growth gains are possible in newly made ponds. With good water, the average small beaver pond may supply upwards of 100 pounds of trout per year for several years. Then the catch tapers off, and at the same time fishing down brook becomes progressively poorer. A brook that apparently contained only native trout begins to show a substantial population of suckers and various minnows. I maintain the beavers are only trying to show us that the same or similar things happen to fish crops as happen on a farm when the same land is planted to the same crop season after season.

Farmers rotate their crops. They know that one crop takes nitrogen from the soil while another crop can replace it. They know that some crops are host to certain diseases while others are immune. They know that some crops compact the soil while others loosen and aerate it. With their knowledge they are able to not only maintain but to continually improve the productivity of their lands. What do we know, for instance, of the possibilities of crop rotation in fish ponds?

I wrote in these columns last year of the placing of rainbow trout fingerlings in an old beaver pond containing a waning population of brook trout. I told how these rainbow trout grew vigorously. They are still growing. Could this be a sort of waterborne adaptation of crop rotation? Many, many tests of this kind will be needed before the effects can be evaluated.

In a bass-bream pond, crappies were added several years ago. The bass and sunfish crop goes on about as usual. The crappies live but just don't grow. Evidently this combination is not quite right. What would happen if the bass-bream pond was drained and perch and crappies substituted? Or a combination of carp and Great Northern Pike? Or suppose the pond was drained and allowed to lie fallow for a year? Or that in the case of one of the many farm ponds now being built in our state, it be drained periodically every three or five years and plowed and planted to onions or celery or some such muckland crop? What effect would this sort of rotation have on the longtime productivity of the water basin?

To these and many other questions we just don't know the best answers. I believe that in the interest of future fishing we ought, all of us, to make a sustained effort to know more about fish life in controlled ponds.

I know that to many Angler readers the ultimate thrill of fresh water fishing is to wade a clear, cold mountain stream, but I also know we have many thousands of fishermen (and women) who prefer still water. Some miles downstream from Emporium, I saw fishermen who ignored trout jumping in the Sinnemahoning, wade it, and climbed the railroad embankment in order to fish a small pond hidden there. There is a measure of peace and contentment to be found in such fishing. It is entirely apart from the rush and tumble of a trout stream that leads you on, and on, and on.

Particularly I would like these quiet anglers, as they fish, to consider the corn field of which I spoke. If it were full of weeds, untended, there would be little corn to call a crop. Clean out the weeds, let the sunshine in, and you will catch more and bigger fish from your pond. I guarantee it. In the valley of the Sinnemahoning and up the Bennett Branch several such weed choked ponds exist. The annual weight of fishes, and the size of individuals caught therein will increase in direct ratio to the energy spent in cleaning out the weeds.

It could be the flashing green and gold of a bigmouth bass is reminiscent of the green and gold of luxuriant corn. I suppose it is. But of one thing any fisherman can be sure, the exploding strike of a big bass is ample reward for many hours of chopping spatterdocks. That I also guarantee.

CHAPTER 26

MUD!

THERE ARE, I SUPPOSE, many, many kinds of mud. Let me be the first to confess, as a nature student, that I traveled a long road down the first half of this twentieth century before I became aware that mud was, or could be, interesting instead of exasperating.

Most of us fishing are prone to accept mud as one of the minor nuisances of the sport, as we accept mosquitos or snags or slippery rocks. But when we stop to think about it, we may realize that mud or muck is nothing more than a combination of soil and water. And soil is the base from which all life springs. Scientists tell us that our lives depend upon grass. Most of us can understand the cycle of mice eating grass roots, and foxes eating mice, so that if there were no grass there could be no foxes.

In fishing the cycle is the same. Grass grows in water or in muck or mud just as it grows on well-drained soil, excepting that the plants have developed different forms and characteristics due to differences in environment. Algae are the common grasses of pond water. And algae are the foundation of grass upon which fish life rests. As with the foxes and the mice, so the bass eats the minnow that ate the insects that fed upon the algae.

Now we know that algae and bacteria cannot grow in pure, that is to say, distilled water. All plants and animals must have food. H2o in itself cannot provide food. It is the medium by which food is carried to and through plants. Thus, the mud along a stream or the muck at the bottom of a pond is the storehouse for the food supply that controls the whole cycle of life in the water. If the storehouse is empty the algae cannot flourish, and the insects will starve, and the minnows and the bass cannot exist. When you get right down to the bottom of it, mud is the stuff that determines the size and quantities of fish we catch.

Now some of the necessary chemicals used by the algae are directly dissolvable into the water, as, for instance, lime. Others, like nitrogen, must be fixed by bacteria before they can be utilized as plant food. Pick up a handful of mud along the water. It doesn't look like much, does it? Yet it is teeming with life. In an ounce of it there may be upwards of 50 million microbes living, eating, dying; each busy at his trade. Some cause decay, and transform dead vegetation into new plant food. But and be sure of it, there are millions of living things in a handful of mud, and they are all busy.

Scientists have discovered that some of the byproducts of the labors of these microbes or molds or fungi are used as drugs. Penicillin was one of the first of several such drugs. Other useful medicines have been discovered, they call these things antibiotics, in the world of teeming life of these soil organisms. Streptomycin, aureomycin, chloromycetin, these new drugs come from some of the millions of unseen living things you may hold in your handful of muck from the water's edge.

As some of you know, I have had a long (and time consuming) interest in beavers and beaver ponds. Originally it was the fish and the fishing that led me to seek out hidden ponds. I soon noticed that wherever the beavers established a colony, it became a sort of focal point for practically all the other wild creatures in the area. And in country where I knew my way around, that is, country I had hunted and fished before the beavers moved in, I became convinced that not only was the new pond a center of activity, but that there was a definite increase in both numbers and vigor among the creatures of the forest living nearby.

Too many times to be coincidence, I noticed increases in the woodcock population, and in ruffed grouse and cottontail rabbits. I've seen colonies of cottontails develop where none had been before. Lately I have discussed these observations with several experienced field men employed by our Pennsylvania Game Commission. They are unanimous in agreeing that pond water is a boon to small game development. Most of them had arrived at this conclusion just as I had, from observation in the field. But we didn't know why.

We were not, however, the only people who questioned these things. Agricultural scientists have been working hand in hand with medical men on this anti-biotic business. They have lately come up with a discovery that ties the whole thing together. They talk about "animal protein factor," the thing that turkeys, chickens and pigs must have to grow strong and healthy. And in this they know of a vitamin (B12) that may revolutionize the whole field of hog and poultry feeding on the farm. This B12 is the thing that controls pernicious anemia in humans. It is present in liver extracts that are used to treat anemia.

These agricultural men knew for a long time that baby chicks grew better on built-up litter, that they got some unknown nutritional factor from the litter or the droppings mixed therein. And they eventually discovered the secret lay in the activities of one of these soil organisms. It was making B12. And B12 was the element in manure, in yeast, and in milk that was giving them rapid growth rates. Now they know how to manufacture B12 in the laboratory and mix it with cheaper feeds to produce heavier and healthier pigs and chickens.

To me, and to the Game Commission men with whom I've discussed this, these things begin to explain why wild life surges upward when a small pond is built in wild land. When I see a cottontail approach a beaver pond in early evening, hop delicately through the mud to the water's edge to drink, and retire to the shelter of a bush and spend ten minutes carefully cleansing his feet with his tongue, I begin to suspect it is all a part of Mother Nature's infinitely accurate plan to give him the vitamins he must have.

Certainly, conditions become ideal for the growth and development of soil organisms in and near the beaver colony. The very nature of the beavers (to be continually dragging wood into the water) is to maintain a food supply not only for themselves but for the minute creatures that attack the wood. As it decays, by action of some of these organisms, food useful to others is released, and so the cycle is begun, to expand outward and upward. As the algae find food in abundance, the insects prosper, and birds including woodcock and ruffed grouse find life rich and interesting. So also, as the waterborne life surges upward, the land animals will benefit from the increased vigor of the grasses.

A beaver pond is rarely a permanent thing. They build, and cut the trees, and move to build again. In a wild remote corner of Clinton County, Pennsylvania there is a wide shallow upland valley where beavers have worked practically undisturbed for almost twenty years. Before they came it was a barren land, sustaining little but stunted stands of poplar and scraggly blueberry bushes. Now there is a wide expanse of fertile land where the wild grass grows shoulder high and small game flourishes.

But with all this we have drifted away from fish and fishing. Many beaver ponds contain fish. And in the northern tier of Pennsylvania counties most of these ponds contain native trout. These trout are not more permanent than the ponds themselves, and they should be harvested.

I find a reluctance on the part of many trout anglers to fish these ponds. The trout are well fed and difficult to catch. They sometimes grow almost unbelievably fast. As long ago as 1937 we found a pond and saw brook trout we estimated to weigh between three and four pounds. We could not land them. We could hook these trout with small wet flies in the late evening, but we never landed one. The pond was a maze of standing timber, so soon as we hooked a fish, he took a half hitch around the nearest tree and departed with the fly.

This pond and these trout have long since disappeared. But there are others. And it is the rich and teeming mud that makes them possible. Long live the beavers!

CHAPTER 27

A Drop of Water

THESE TWO OLD MEN were camping and fishing on Sandy Creek, in Mercer County, one day in July. Age is naturally relative. Even so, both these men were well past the ordinary age for retirement. They were of that age of man from whom all bitterness has been filtered through the sands of time.

They had been on a vacation, they said, ever since trout season opened. They had a battered sedan rigged for camping with a built-in double bunk. And with a gasoline cookstove, plus a mountain of assorted camping and fishing gear, they were in truth vacationing. Nearly three months they had lived aboard that car, they said, fishing where and when they pleased. I gathered it was the vacation of a life-time.

We talked of brooks and creeks and rivers and fish. Yes, they had fished the Kettle. And First Fork. He caught a 13 1/2-inch fallfish in First Fork. No, they had not seen the First Fork in all the forty years it was polluted. But they had seen the Clarion this summer. Yes, it was like that, maybe worse.

When I mentioned a tiny beaver pond set high along a forest road between Cross Forks and Wharton, they knew it. We stayed there, they told me. It's cram-jammed full of little trout. And they said they would have stayed there longer only they ran shy of grub.

A picture of these two aged happy fishermen has crossed my mind many times since we chatted that midsummer day in Mercer County. They had stood on the rim of the Canyon of Pine Creek and looked far. And then camped in the valley and caught some fish. Now, finally, the reason I kept thinking about these two old fellows is clear. It was not an accident they were able to travel so widely, camp where it pleased them, and fish a beaver pond cram-jammed with little trout! Certainly, they could not have had their vacation so easily a generation ago.

If you could only step backward, say, twenty-five years. Maybe I can explain it best by saying we had practically no roads in the mountains twenty-odd years ago. There was good fishing in the Kettle Creek country a quarter century ago. And a few dozen fishermen. There are thousands of fishermen in that country today, fishing the same waters. And the fishing is good. Fifty mile an hour highways span the hill country. Now great forests cover all that north central section. A quarter of a century ago we hunted deer in open barrens where they jumped and ran like rabbits through clipped pasture grass. But lately the forests are grown. The hills are covered. And the reason we have those forests lies principally in the foresight that established a network of fire towers scattered far across the state of Pennsylvania.

Roads and forest fire prevention are not the only things that made it possible for our two old friends to enjoy their vacation of a lifetime. Call it symbolic if you like, the fact remains that a good and great amount of work has been done toward repairing and improving the Pennsylvania we inherited.

There were Game Commission men farsighted enough to buy land, establish refuges, restock beavers and other animals; and to spend millions of manhours of labor to make Pennsylvania a better vacation land. Consider also the work accomplished by Fish Commission men in these past years. So, it goes, from Secretary of Highways to maintenance crew workers, from Game Commissioner to common laborer, from Fish Commissioner to sportsman engaged in a stream improvement project, and from Department of Forests and Waters to Highway Police, hundreds of men and women have worked over the years, worked perhaps unknowingly, to plan the perfect vacation for two old fellows who deserved it. And whom, whoever they are and wherever they may be, appreciate every bit of it. I like to think of it that way.

So, you see, in spite of the bickering and the squabbling that sometimes seems to rule our affairs, we are on the right and the good trail, and we are gaining on the main goal. I like to think that every man working for Pennsylvania was directly helping our two old friends to totter safely along the vacation path they had chosen. That hundreds of men had and were helping to smooth the path for their treble old car. And other hundreds had planted the fish they were able to catch. And the many more who were engaged in caring for the wild birds and animals they saw were also helping. We saw a bear in Potter County.

The main goal is clear. Simply that Pennsylvania be a better place to live in. Also, to respect the right of each individual to his freedom. And whether he be young and strong, or aged and feeble, to protect and enrich the Pennsylvania he calls home. Our state, you must understand, is first of all its People.

Now about the drop of water. Without it there would be no Commonwealth of Pennsylvania. We could hardly exist without raindrops. We have been altogether too careless about water, and how we used it. Because rain fell in abundance, we thought we could afford to be careless. We wasted water. The time is rapidly approaching, however, when there won't be enough clean water to fill the need. In some sections that time is already upon us.

As anglers, we are already feeling the pinch. Industrial and mine acid wastes shut us off many miles of streams. We crowd onto the unpolluted streams. And land owners who were tolerant of occasional fishermen are increasingly posting land against our increasing crowds. A good share of the waters flowing through public lands, that is, State Game Lands or State Forests, are polluted by privately owned mines or industries. All this has come about, and come onto us sometimes swiftly, simply because we had water in abundance, and were careless.

The unfortunate phase of the whole situation is that water owns an inherited tendency to run downhill. Carelessness in waste disposal by one may cause loss or damage to others many miles removed. And since it has been the custom in our country to dispose of waste via the "water runs downhill" system for so very many years, a good bit of opposition develops whenever corrective measures are proposed.

Sometimes, though, opposition is a good thing. It helps clarify the situation. I think it is plainly evident to anyone who travels widely in Pennsylvania that those valleys wherein the waters are polluted are neither so well kept or prosperous or so productive as is the case where pollution is at a minimum. There is a lesson in this fact. If Pennsylvania is to continue to attract new industry and to grow in population, it must either find new valleys or clean up the polluted ones. Clean new land does not roll off assembly lines like new automobiles. It's up to us to make the best of what we already have. It is all we will ever get.

Now the role of the licensed fisherman in the furtherance of a Clean Streams program is, as I see it, twofold. In the first place, because he owns a very personal interest in fish and fishing, any progress in pollution abatement will benefit him immediately and directly. Perhaps the best way the average man can assist this effort is to support his local sportsmen's club. The day has come when any political candidate worthy of the name stands ready to appear before his district sportsmen's organization to answer their questions and seek their approval of his candidacy. He will, that is, if the meetings are well attended by voters. In almost any district in Pennsylvania the sportsmen's vote, solidly assembled, can make or break the candidate. We ought to remember that.

The angler's second duty, and I put it second not because it is of less importance, is to look out for the little things. We are not a passel of angels, we fishermen, and we have spoiled a lot of fishing scenery ourselves. The broken bottles, the tin cans, defunct auto tires, and other offensive debris, are, in large part, our own doing. In some cases, I know, they have been our undoing, for they have caused "No Trespassing" signs to bloom where none had bloomed before. This is no time to say, "I didn't do it", this is the time to clean up the mess. I admit it is not so much fun to pulverize a broken bottle or bury a tin can as it is to catch a trout, but I believe that if we do it, and continue to do it, we will profit by it. In the name of common honesty, while we are pressing for more and more Clean Streams, we should set our own house in order.

CHAPTER 28

Our Northern Pike

WHENCE CAME THE GREAT Northern Pike we have been catching with increasing frequency in northwest Pennsylvania? Ten years ago, we neither saw nor caught Esox Lucius in the Allegheny River or in French Creek (variously called Frenchmen's Creek or Le Boeuf's River). Nor did we catch these fish in the lower reaches of Big Sandy Creek in Venango County at that time.

In the summer of 1938, while prospecting a swampy stretch of Big Sandy Creek above Raymilton, I was caught in a sudden and drenching thunderstorm. I remember vividly being equipped with a light seven-and-a-half-foot fly rod and some bass size streamer flies. After the storm I encountered the pike. It was a thrilling experience. Here was a fish I had never before caught. And it was fast and furious action in the two hours between storm and nightfall.

Those fish were not exceptionally large, though somewhat longer than the smallmouth bass ordinarily present in such waters. They ran between 18 and 20 inches long. There seemed to be an endless supply of them. And though I could not positively identify them, I did not let that fact spoil my fun. The fish struck with a savage killing fury and jumped like tormented demons.

I soon learned they did not fight like smallmouth bass or brook trout, with an all-out effort, but would intersperse bursts of energy with long pauses of inaction. And that, though you could lead them almost at will with the light fly rod you never could anticipate the instant the frenzy might be resumed.

Another thing I learned, and quickly, was that beside having tooth and jaw structure almost exactly like the muskellunge, these fish had several assorted razor blades built into their gill covers. And these could cut your hand sharply as you struggled to hold the fish in order to get the hook away from his mouth.

I emerged from the evening's excitement with both hands cut and bleeding, and at the same time tremendously excited over catching this, to me at least, new and savage fish.

A few days later Game Commissioner Lamberton went with me to the creek. He, having had considerable experience as a Canadian fisherman, was able to identify the fish as Great Northern Pike, and also to point out the low opinion many people had of the species.

Low opinion of others or not, I knew I had had fast and furious action with these slim and vicious fishes, and I kept hunting and fishing for them. I finally caught one longer than the 22-inch size limit (at that time) and cooked and ate it. The flavor was almost exactly as local muskellunge, and we liked it. Some don't.

As the years passed the fish became more and more numerous. We caught more and larger specimens, and we began to catch them in the Allegheny and in French Creek. They have multiplied enormously in the last dozen years, and so, I can assure you, has the angling fraternity multiplied in pursuit.

Shortly after Commissioner Lamberton identified the pike I showed one to my grandfather, who had done his boyhood fishing along South Sandy Creek in what is now Game Lands No. 39. He said he had speared such fish as a boy, and they had called them 'grass pike'. And the reason, he thought, the name had stuck in his memory was because there wasn't any grass growing in South Sandy Creek when he was a boy in the 1870's. It had then been 60 or 65 years since he had seen such a fish. If he was correct, and the fish were the same, then it would appear these fish have always been native to these parts. This seemed entirely possible, since Esox Lucius is one of the world's most widely distributed fishes, according to the encyclopedia.

Not long ago, however, Warden 'Rosey' White, well known to most western Pennsylvania sportsmen, unearthed some scraps of evidence to the effect that these fish were introduced, as fry or fingerlings, into the upper reaches of Big Sandy Creek, near the town of Sandy Lake, in the early years of this century. The story goes that the young fish were brought in by rail, and stocked by members of a now defunct sportsmen's club of that city.

Warden White was engrossed with the same question that was in my mind. Why, if these fish have always been native to Big Sandy Creek, or were stocked there nearly fifty year ago, did they lie dormant for so many years and then all at once begin to grow and multiply and expand their territory? The answer to that question, I think, lies in a little noticed change that has taken place in these waters, plus a habit of the Great Northern Pike themselves.

In the early days, grist mills and water power were the common thing throughout Pennsylvania. Big Sandy Creek was well supplied with mill dams at Pecan, Polk, Raymilton, Reed's Furnace and Sandy Lake. French Creek had a substantial dam at its very mouth in Franklin. I believe these dams prevented the free migration of many fishes, and that, with lighter lures as well as the heavier ones, you would do well to carry an extra line.

For night fishing, or for just getting in and out of an out-of-the-way fishing spot back in the brush before or after daylight hours, a good flashlight is a friend in need. If you have need for a flashlight, there is always a good chance that you will have need for extra batteries or an extra bulb. I always carry all three.

A good grade of machine oil has a rightful place in anyone's tackle box. The manufacturers of reels recommend a drop of oil at the crucial points of wear before each fishing trip. You can't forget to oil your reel if you carry your oil with you. Or maybe the outboard motor needs a few drops. If you happen to drop your reel in dirty water or sand, it might need a thorough cleaning. And, after cleaning, it takes oil.

An extra roll of film, or film pack, may make the trip for you. More than once I have come home from a successful fishing excursion without any fish. It was the picture of Ed losing the big one, a buck drinking at the water's edge, a flock of ducks that allowed us to approach close enough for a good picture or some other equally interesting shot that gave me my money's worth. If one of the opportunities comes up just after you have finished the last shot on the film in the camera, extra film becomes a much-needed must.

That fish scale? Well, being a fisherman, I know that I'm entitled to exaggerate some without actually being called a liar. But I don't like to do it. I like to know just how heavy the big ones are after they are caught. That little scale is quite accurate, and it gets checked once in a while just to make sure. Since it is impractical to carry a fish home without removing the insides, I like to take their weight as soon as they are caught to compare them with ones caught before. If everyone would check their fish the same way, we wouldn't hear about so many big ones reported from someone's imagination, and fellows like you and me wouldn't be so hard pressed trying to keep up with them.

That old bandanna handkerchief has a multitude of uses. You can use it to wipe your hands after catching a fish and not run so much risk of losing your casting rod on the next heave with slippery fingers. It can be used to dry lures before returning them to the tackle box, to wipe off your fly rod before placing it back in its case, or as a temporary bandage if your knife slips. If the big one gets away, you can use it to dry your tears.

All of the above items are ones that I believe that every angler should carry in his tackle box in one form or another. They have proven their value many times over for me, and I sincerely believe that you will, or have, found a use for all of them at one time.

These to me are the musts. One tool omitted, because I carry it in my fishing jacket, is a tiny screw driver. It is invaluable when it becomes necessary to take apart a reel or work on some of your lures. You can obtain one with a pencil clip such as I have or one of the little combination sets that fit several screw drivers compactly within a case only as large as the handle on the largest screw driver.

In addition to all these, I also carry a small wrench for the outboard, extra shear pins, stringer, hook extractor, single edge razor blades and anything else that I think I might need.

I have the same number of useless plugs and spoons and assorted junk lures that I carry around the country the same as you do, but I'd part with any or all of them before I'd be caught on an extended fishing trip without any of my "tackle box extras."

CHAPTER 29

The Last Day

IT IS THE LAST day of July and hot. Over here in Pennsylvania our trout season closes with the last day of July. Borrowing a phrase from the kids, I'll give you three guesses as to what I am doing this sultry afternoon. Right the first time—trout fishing. I might add, borrowing further from the kids, that I am playing hookey.

But that is something of a debatable point, playing hookey to go fishing on the last day. Accidents sometimes happen. The game of life must go on, and who can know whether this is the last day of the season or the last day of his whole fishing career?

Why am I in such a mood, with the sky so brilliantly blue, the sun white and hot, and with each tiny breeze so wonderfully refreshing, I do not know. I do know, however, that every detail of that day is so deeply etched, so photographically welded into my memory, that I shall carry it always. And if it should so happen that a man became bedfast in his declining years, he could fish this day over and over again in the endless, sleepless nights. He could fish again a thousand times—yes, ten thousand times. Such are the dividends of trout fishing.

It is high noon when I reach the stream. And if the day is beautifully clear, it is also seasonally hot. This is a fish-straight-through- trip, no walking back, so Mrs. Blair drops me off at the bridge with the understanding that I will appear at a friend's house in the village by dusk or shortly thereafter.

The car departs, and I am alone with nearly five miles of trout water to negotiate in nine hours. Is it virgin water? I should say not. In the clearing by the bridge lays the scattered debris of many fishing parties. Pittsburgh is about sixty miles due south. She can send forth a regular army of fishermen on Opening Day. I've mingled with them. They are a bunch of real people. But all is quiet and deserted now. I sneak down the path toward the big pool below the bridge. I see a trout—and he sees me, too!

I wonder how many fishermen he has seen this year, and I can imagine. Here a few days prior to season's opening, I had watched at least two hundred "fresh from the hatchery" trout fanning in the slow current. One remains! I mentally doff my hat to him. What a gauntlet he has survived— the last of the Mohicans, indeed! You walk with God, my friend. I'll not harm you. So, I move on downstream.

On a sand bar I see man tracks, but they are old. Two or three days, I guess. I work along, watching, looking, not fishing hard. This is the hard-fished water for a mile or so below the bridge. Most fishermen working diligently for an hour or two, then turn back. That's the one good thing about this brook, there aren't any roads. It's a long stretch from the bridge to the village, and not many men fish clear through. Sure enough, I see where the last man had turned back upstream.

As I continue, I speculate about him. He was a big man, a heavy one. He had caught no trout. I would bet on that for he had walked right up to the pools, as if daring the trout to strike. You can do that in April, with a roily steam, but not in July with low, clear water. He had waded, too, and that just isn't done in the best trout stalking circles, in July.

So, I keep moving down with the tinkling, crystal current. Now the sand bars are trampled with deer tracks, and the baby feet of raccoons. I begin to see some trout and to fish a little, without success.

Soon I had come to the pool where I had heard Bill swear so mightily one spring morning. Was that six or seven years ago? No matter, it was a big trout, and it got away. I sneak. I carefully inspect the 3X leader—debate on changing it—decide to gamble—and flip the tiny dry Black Gnat onto the swift water.

A flashing iridescent splash—he's got it! But he is only a slim six incher. You are a game one, little fellow. Back you go to rest awhile. And tell the Old One, Bill won't be back next spring. He's fishing with St. Peter nowadays.

Another mile and the valley widens. A tiny brook joins the main stream. The water is brown from beaver workings. I sneak through the alders to the dam. Everything is swampy. The mosquitoes rise in swarms. It's almost unbearably hot. The water is dark, like stale coffee. Everything is tangled, rotting. I cast. A minnow drowns the fly. I return to the main stream and travel on.

I notice my shadow for the first time. It is growing longer. It is mid-afternoon by now, and a precious little breeze makes me hope it is growing cooler.

A little way further, and I can see the top of the old iron furnace. It is a massive structure of sandstone blocks, watching here alone beside the stream. Alone, yes, and a long time alone. I'm told these iron furnaces were built between 1840 and 1850, and this is 1948. So, what are a hundred years?

This quiet, deserted valley must have been a busy place when you were built, Mr. Furnace. How many men—how many sweating horses worked to build you here? It is of no importance now. The clearing is choked with poplar and wild apple thickets, and the roads are overgrown.

I wonder about the trout fishing here a hundred years ago? Were the trout as wild—as wary—then? Precious little can you find of fishing in the records these men left. Were they so furious in their efforts to conquer that land that they took no time to fish? It doesn't matter now. They are gone, Mr. Furnace, and you are here, alone. Their roads, their fields, their ambitions, now are all but lost in the swiftly growing forest.

With all of this I am still a fisherman. My eyes squint instinctively as they rove the sun-brilliant facets of trout brook water, and just as instinctively my fly seeks the likely runs and pockets. The stream is larger now and falling more swiftly.

Now we are down to bedrock. The water tumbles laughingly. Hemlocks shade the moss-grown rocks, and it is cooler, I think. I stop to rest and change my fly. There is no hatch over the water nor any trout in my creel.

The Black Gnat is set aside. A big bushy Queen of the Waters gets the nod. I shorten the leader to 1X. A big fly will only tie knots in a 3X tippet. I am going to catch a trout. And I do!

The fly-toe dances on the water, and there is an instant silver flash. The slack line zings through my fingers. The real wails like a fire siren calling all hands to impending disaster. Stop screaming, I'm wide awake!

Forty feet away the water breaks, and a trout bursts out in an insanely wild leap. He lands broadside on a mid-stream rock. It only changes his direction! Down over the rocks he goes, through the snowy foam, into the pool. Motion ceases. All is calm.

I tread warily. A brook trout fights doggedly, determined to win his hiding place. A brown trout fights cannily, intelligently. But the rainbow goes insane.

We don't get many rainbows in western Pennsylvania, except pond raised hatchery fish. But once in a while you hook into one who has been out on his own for a year or two, and when you do, your first reaction is to become a little dubious of Henshall's a "pound for pound, and inch for inch". Then again, you hook a smallmouth, and the thunder of his splashing makes you forget the forked-lightning insanity of the rainbow trout. Eventually, I creel him.

I think it is growing dusk here in the shade of the hemlocks. I kill a good solid brown trout before I come out into open country. It is suddenly quiet again as the brook ceases tumbling and swims leisurely through the lowlands.

The heat is once more oppressive. When I look up to check the sun, I see the thunder clouds piling over it. For the first time, because the brook is quiet, I hear their distant rumbling. Now it dawns on me why the birds are silent, why the air is still and heavy, and why the heat is oppressive. A thunder storm is coming. I hurry on. Trout don't strike right before a storm, I say. But two just did, so I slow down and fish some more.

Thunder is distinct and disturbing now. The sun is blotted out. I haven't far to go—a mile or so. There is one last good pool here. It is deep and shaded. This is really trout headquarters. They winter here. There is food aplenty all the time. There is a long shallow riffle above the pool open to the sun. It is not paved with shifting, rolling gravel, but with angular fragments of lime rock. Tiny caddis worms spread their nets by the millions through the winter months. It is their pasture ground.

There we have it. A trout brook needs cover, yes; but it must have food producing areas as well. Let the sunlight in on the shallow aerated water. Let the microscopic algae flourish. Let the nymphs feed on the herbage, and the trout will grow long and fat and self-reliant.

The pool is hemmed with outward thrusting branches. It is shaded and doubly dark today because of the black clouds above. The thunder crashes strongly. There is a symphony of sound. The flute-like rippling of the shallow riffles, the mysterious strings of the deep, dark pool, the powerful crashing of the giant drums above, and the solid silence of the electrostatic atmosphere—all speed a pounding tempo in my heart.

See here, this is no awesome Amazonian jungle! This is only a crystal-clear trout brook in Pennsylvania. A thunderstorm will clear the air. A wetting won't hurt you. You are soaked with sweat already.

I lay a Queen out on the water. It is like a sheet of polished glass. The rain descends. No foolin'. A few huge drops fall like pistol bullets on the water. The gates are opened. The rain pours down. It is icy down my back. I shift my hat brim and stand close and small as possible. After the first chilling shock has passed, I am wonderfully refreshed. I look for the Queen. She is gone—drowned in the downpour.

There is a tug on the line as I begin to lift it. I tug too. I see a flash of red-gold deep through the rain-pocked water. He fights furiously, but he is small. I net a brilliant bluegill.

Look here, little fellow, you are lost. This is brown trout water. You belong in a lazy pond, not here in this cold-water brook. He won't answer. He's gorged the fly, and it has cut his gill. His blood streams out across my hand. His life is done already.

I cut the fly out. It is soaked and slimed. I can't dry it. The rain is pouring down. I cast my wet-dry fly. It sinks. I cannot see it, but there is a dull flash in the water. I strike instinctively. Wow! This fish has power. He is strong. We fight.

How long do we struggle? Three minutes—or five minutes—or ten—time concerns us not. He bores deep. I am in to my boot-tops at the edge of the pool. The rain slackens, and I can see a little beneath the surface of the water. The bamboo is relentless. He is coming up. I see him. He is a trout!

Of course, I am excited. I fumble the net. I miss. He is really frightened now. We have it out between us. I collect the fragments of my calm composure, and this time I get him in the net. He is a "keeper". I crack him on the skull and bend him into the basket. To prove how calm and collected I am at a time like this, I fastened the lid—securely!

I cast again. The fly sinks. The flash—I strike. Another "keeper". Down he goes toward the bottom. I believe he is heavier than the other. I am more confident now. I fight calmly and net him neatly. He is a little longer than the other, half an inch, perhaps. I kill him.

The basket lid is tied shut with string in case the first trout should regain consciousness. I heave the second one into the woods. I'll retrieve him later. I'm a busy man right now!

Out goes the fly again with a short roll cast. It sinks, oh, so slowly. The rain has passed. The pool is leaden. The hour is growing late. Mist is rising everywhere. The thunder crashes and re-echoes in the main valley half a mile away. Time is racing now. A moment ago, it stood still. There was no such thing as time. Can Einstein explain this? The fly sags slowly in the dark water. I can barely follow it with my eye. So, I twitch it a tiny bit—"the better to see you, my dear".

He comes straight up. I see him—each orange fin, every colored spot on his twisting side, he is brilliant in the water. Eternity is an instant. He turns straight down. I strike—snap! He is lost in the depths.

The fault is my own. I rail out at Fate. Then I am ashamed. The forest is so quiet, the very air so pure and clean. Who am I to defile it? The leader knot should have been tested. It had been through two good battles. So, it failed in the supreme moment. How big was he? He was too big for my worn leader.

I have held the heft of him up beside a yardstick to estimate his length, I have fondled him in my mind, and I have mentally examined the savage graceful hook of his under-jaw as it turned in the water. How big is he? He is big enough to fill my pleasant dreams for many years to come.

But it is growing late. I must hurry on. It will soon be dark, and I have no light. The mist is like fog. The sun is long gone. Trout season is finished!

I press into the dripping bushes and search around the litter. I find the second trout. He is plastered with dead leaves and is growing still already. I rinse him tenderly, pluck a dripping fern, and arrange him with the others in the willow basket.

As I go down the valley in peace, through the dripping underbrush, my thoughts begin to sober. The intoxication of conquest has passed, the Last Day is nearly done, and all at once I am acutely conscious of weary muscles and gnawing hunger.

Finally, I am scrambling up the railroad embankment, through the tangled blackberry canes (I've mislaid the path in the night) holding my precious fly rod high and safe. It is black-dark as I step out onto the tracks. Faint flashes show in the eastern sky. The storm is far away, muttering, as I stumble along the invisible railroad ties.

Ten minutes, or twenty minutes in this muggy carboniferous night, will put me under the village street light. Soon I will be home, in dry clothing, and leaning on the kitchen table. The coffee pot will be bubbling, the bacon spattering, and I will be telling about my fishing trip.

So, I trudge up the track, one tie for each weary step—and plan the tale I will tell, of the mighty battle with the Big One, and how he won it—neglecting all mention, of course, of the worn leader or of my splintered composure.

This is the way of fishermen. But Peter was a fisherman—comes my turn, I think he'll understand.

CHAPTER 30

It Happened This Way

OVER THE YEARS, DAD had discovered the great fishing in Canadian lakes. The June fishing trip to Canada had become an annual event. His fishing buddies, Louie, Glenn, and Joe, would travel with him on these Canadian trips whenever they could get the time off work. Of course, Dad had always worked for himself, so he could take off and go fishin' whenever the itch became too great to ignore.

A few days before the latest planned trip, Dad came down with the flu. At least that's what he thought it was. His doctor set up an appointment at the hospital to get some tests done, just to be sure it wasn't anything serious. But after a couple days in bed, Dad was feeling much better. The day he was to go to the hospital for the tests, he left for Canada instead.

On this trip, Joe was his fishing companion. While Dad and Joe were loading the station wagon for the trip, Mom protested his leaving. I can still hear Dad say, "Honey, I'll be fine. I'll get those tests done when I get back."

Mom got a call from Dad when they arrived. Then a few days later Joe called to say that Dad was in the hospital. Seems he got the flu again, or so he thought, and had spent a couple days in the cabin in bed. When he wasn't feeling better, Joe took him to the hospital in a nearby town. The doctor said that Dad had had a heart attack, but he was doing better. Joe drove the station wagon home to pick Mom and me up, then drove us back to the hospital in Canada to be with Dad.

When we arrived, Dad was in good spirits. The hospital specialized in heart and lung conditions. The staff were taking very good care of him. Joe helped us get settled into a bed and breakfast place within walking distance of the hospital. Every day Mom and I would walk to the hospital and spend the day with Dad. Mom and Dad would talk, read the paper, and sometimes just sit quietly together, she in the chair, and he in his bed.

I would usually go downstairs to the waiting room where I could read magazines and watch some TV. It was June 12, 1963. I had just turned fourteen years old and had an interest in the fan magazines of the day. Engrossed in an article, I was startled by my Mom's voice, "Donna, come here right now." She was standing on the stairs looking pale and shaking. Dad had just had another heart attack. A nurse hurried us into a nearby room, telling us to wait there. It seemed like ages, but the doctor finally came in to say that Dad was gone.

Mom made arrangements for Dad's body to be taken by train to Toronto. Mom and I rode in a sleeping car. I remember sleeping in the top bunk, or rather trying to sleep. Neither one of us got much sleep. I just remember hearing Mom crying in the bunk below me.

The local funeral home in Franklin sent a hearse and a limousine to meet us at the train station. I remember looking at the hearse in front of us as we rode home to Franklin, Pennsylvania. It was a very quiet trip.

There were lots of people at the funeral. Everyone loved my dad. It felt like all of Franklin came to pay their respects. He was well known and loved by many. But I think Joe said it best when he said that Dad passed while on a fishing trip, doing what he loved to do. One could say that he was playin' hookey again that day. As Dad would say, "This is the way of fishermen." But, like Dad said, Peter was a fisherman. I like to think that when Peter met Dad at the Pearly Gates, he understood and said, "Welcome Don. Let's go fishin.'"

www.ingramcontent.com/pod-product-compliance
Lightning Source LLC
Chambersburg PA
CBHW052109090426
42741CB00009B/1743